Compelled

What others are saying about "Compelled"

"Compelled" is a timely book birthed from a deep sense of calling and passion. Dr. Grover provides a book firmly rooted in the Bible, practical in contemporary application, and immensely 'user friendly' as a reference. Human Trafficking is very disturbing. "Compelled" outlines substantive hope. It is a must for every individual or community organization seeking to understand and make a tangible difference to eradicate modern day slavery.

Dr. Jeff Johnson
Senior Pastor, FBC Commerce, Texas
President, BGCT

"Compelled" by Dr. T.L. Grover is a terrific resource to help today's Christian understand their contribution to human trafficking as well as help them learn how to become engaged in the fight to stop this form of modern day slavery. It belongs in the library of anyone serious about impacting the social issue of our day.

Jeff Barrows, D.O., M.A.
VP of Education and Advocacy
Director, Abolition International Shelter Association

Want to combat human trafficking? Then DO it! Tomi Grover has offered a plethora of resources which can help everyone to get involved. Providing a Biblical foundation, she lists information for those who want to 'dive in completely'—or begin by 'sticking their toes in the water.' Prayerfully read—and then prayerfully act!!!

Dr, Rev. Lauran Bethell
International Consultant,
International Ministries, ABC/USA

Compelled

Dr. Tomi Grover

Compelled

Author: Tomi Grover

Published by Austin Brothers Publishing

Keller, Texas

www.austinbrotherspublishing.com

ISBN 978-0-9891027-2-8

Copyright © 2013 by Tomi Grover

This and other books published by Austin Brothers Publishing can be purchased at www.austinbrotherspublishing.com

Printed in the United States of America

2013 -- First Edition

Dedication

First, I would like to remember the countless victims especially those whose voices will never be heard. Second, I have deep appreciation for those victims who have had the courage to speak up after being freed and who have become victors and voices for others.

I am privileged to have had the opportunity to meet some amazing adults who have lived to tell their story. Given Kachepa is an exceptional young man with whom I have co-presented on several occasions along with his adoptive "mom" Sandy Shepherd. Mariam Kagaso, who speaks boldly and prophetically. Theresa Flores and Holly Smith are voices for victims and exhibit incredible courage and resilience.

Thirdly, this book is dedicated to all of those compelled to respond to the call of God on their lives—those that were ruined to do anything else with their lives and with whom I stand shoulder to shoulder everyday in prayer and dedication to the cause of Christ to set the captives free.

Finally, to the One who freed me, the Giver of my call to be a watchman on the wall. With a special thanks to Him for a family who always supports my endeavors even if they have their suspicions about my sanity.

Contents

Acknowledgements

While there are many books written about human trafficking,* this work is purposed to address and challenge the Christian church in the US context about its role, responsibility, and response to human trafficking. This book will emphasize practical theology, revealing from the Scriptures (the Christian Bible) God's calling of Christians to respond to trafficking. This book is neither a complete theological discussion nor an exegesis of all the relevant information concerning slavery in the Bible. I leave that work to Bible scholars and experts.

My hope and prayer for this book is that when you read it you will be able to see God's activities in the world concerning human trafficking more clearly and begin exploring your "burning bush call" to be a part of His response. First, you will be challenged to consider the "why" questions of your role, responsibility, and response in human trafficking. Second, we will consider the "what" of the role, responsibility, and response to human trafficking. The possible strategic responses will focus on the four PIER areas (prevention, intervention, education, and restoration). We will also look at "Rules of Engagement" as a means of a decision-making matrix of HOPE.

May this work end up in the hands of Christians, Pastors, and teachers who will help others know of God's compassionate response on the issue and the Church's role, responsibility, and response in human trafficking.

If you will do only one thing with this book, please make it a matter of prayer. Circle the issue of human trafficking in your mind with a bright red marker as an issue you pray over regularly. Read "The Circle Maker" by Mark Batterson to see what a difference encircling the complex issues of human trafficking with prayer will make.

* A selection of those books I recommend is included in the bibliography. For those of you in the US context I highly recommend," The Slave Next Door" by Kevin Bales and Ron Soodalter. This book will

give you a good look at the history of slavery in the United States. They look at the complex issues of modern-day slavery and tell the stories of victims of human trafficking in the United States and the response through the United States government.

Other books on sex trafficking and commercial sexual exploitation of children are available: "In Our Backyard" by Nita Belles, "Not in my Town," Burroughs and Dillon, "Renting Lacy," by Linda Smith of Shared Hope, "The Slave Across the Street," by Theresa Flores, and "Escaping the Devil's Bedroom" by Dawn Herzog Jewel.

Introduction

Human trafficking is the exploitation of people by elements of force, fraud, or coercion in either the labor industry or the commercial sex industry. Research indicates that there are an estimated 27 million people enslaved around the world today. As hard to believe as it is, there are more people enslaved now than during the 350 years of the Trans-Atlantic slave trade.

Anyone who has access to read this, who lives and functions in this modern world, participates by commission or omission in what is happening around the world concerning modern day slavery. This is the issue of our day that all of us contribute to in some form, often without a clue.

Perhaps you do not believe that you add to the problem. Quick test: without looking, where was your shirt made? Would it bother you to know that a worker was exploited to make the price point demanded for that garment? Do you know where the coffee you drank with breakfast was harvested and if the folks that touched the beans were paid a livable wage? Have you eaten chocolate this week? Would it bother you to know that most of the chocolate produced in the world comes from exploited children forced to harvest the cocoa pods? It is very likely these children will never taste chocolate in their lifetime.

Our food, our tangible products, our demand for goods and services—at the lowest possible price—all are a part of the complicated equation called labor trafficking. About half of those enslaved are in labor industries. The likelihood is great that you have something you have purchased that has the fingerprints of someone who has been enslaved in the process of its production.

Forced labor is sometimes hidden in plain sight. Less than 1% of victims are ever rescued according to the United Nations' research. Slavery can be found in restaurants, construction, and labor-intensive jobs or even in a touring choir at your church.

Members of the First Baptist Church in Colleyville, Texas, discovered a Baptist pastor had recruited boys in Zambia to be in a touring choir. The boys were promised that money would be sent to their village to help their families and community with education. They were to be educated in the United States while on tour. Their hopes, dreams, aspirations, and talents had made them easy prey for a greedy trafficker.

The boys experienced broken promises and crushed dreams. Most of them were returned home, shamed in their communities by the trafficker while others stayed in the US to work with government officials. I will share the story of one of these young men, Given Kacepha, in detail later in this work. It has been related in many news stories as well as through the national Rescue and Restore campaign. The best news about Given's story is the greater good that came from his victimization that now affords him an opportunity to make a difference concerning human trafficking.

The commercial sex industry accounts for the other half of those enslaved. Millions of human beings forced to provide sex for sale. About half of all those victimized are children. The demand for sexual services in the world is part of a phenomenon of sexual perversity, pederasty, pedophilia, pornography, and forced prostitution. The proliferation of this demand is fueled by silence about sexual abuse and cultural normalization of engagement of children in sexual behaviors. Children are hyper-sexualized by media, music, clothing, and exposed early and often to pornography. The greatest demand in the porn industry is for children in high sadomasochistic pornography.

At this point, you may be convinced you do not contribute to sex trafficking. Checked off in your mind how you do not contribute?

- I don't buy sex abroad
- I don't abuse or buy children
- I don't buy porn

Contributions to sex trafficking by most citizens are not proactive consumption in the commercial sex industry. Our current culture is more easily entangled by the subtle contributions. Some of those toxic culture factors include music, movies, clothing choices/sexualized fashion, and tolerance of pornography on the web or in commodification of sex for sale. If you think it is not affecting you, consider how many sexualized images are bombarding you every day from the news to the television shows.

These same influences are surrounding children who think that they need the latest fashion including tattoos to make them popular or "in" at school. A desire to fit in or have a cool tattoo changed one child's life forever.

Thirteen-year-old Elisa was active in church, a beautiful eighth grader who was in the gifted and talented program in public school. She was upset with her parents one evening as she went to a basketball game at school. Her girlfriend listened as she berated her parents for not allowing her to get a tattoo. A young man in his 20's overheard her conversation and offered to place a tattoo on the back of her neck under her hair. "Your parents will never know, and we'll have you back before the game is over," he promised.

She made a decision that was not wise and left with two young men she did not know. Her life changed dramatically with the closing of the van door. Elisa was raped by the men and put out at a shopping center. Another man convinced her he would help her. He sold her for sex out of a local motel to more men than she could count. Nyquil was used to help her cope with the pain of being repeatedly raped. Somehow, someone recognized she was in a dangerous situation and took her home. Most girls who are trafficked in the US do not have the fortune of being rescued by a compassionate stranger. The number of US children tricked, trapped, and traded into the commercial sex industry is staggering and exasperating.

Why This Book and Why Now?

The car was stuffed with luggage and four kids who demanded a pit stop. We ventured across Colorado on our annual summer trek despite the news on the radio of reported fires west of our location. We eventually made our stop while the smoke billowed in the distance. I had no worries about the fire. The reports had given no indication the fires were headed our way.

Everyone piled out of the car. I pumped gas, while my family went inside. Far off to the west, I could see the clouds of smoke above the ridgeline. It seemed like such a distant event. I checked the progress on the gas going into the car. Impatient, I took a sighing breath and noticed the smell of smoke in the air.

I glanced again toward the ridge and did a double take. Smoke eclipsed by surreal towering flames twice the height of the trees. I knew the trees had to be 100 feet tall. The flames were a leaping inferno over the ridge. The winds ferociously blew the fire across the mountain directly toward us. The image of the flame blower in the circus spewing out fire from his mouth came to mind. I could feel my stomach knotting up.

The sudden physical anxiety I felt for my family seemed incalculable. I looked down urging the pump to go more quickly. My eyes glimpsed toward my wife and four children emerging from the gas station. Frantically, I waved them toward the car. "Quick, get in the car," I barked. I decided the gas tank was full enough and I felt shaky as I put the hose back on the pump. My thoughts immediately focused on protecting my wife and kids.

My heart raced as I jumped into the car nearly out of breath. "Everyone buckled up?" I asked.

Five yeses checked off in my mind. Quickly we drove back to Interstate 25 and headed south out of town. Blaring sirens of fire trucks and patrol cars whizzed by us. We passed the intersection just before our turn toward the next destination. In the rearview mirror, we could see the Highway Patrol blocking the interstate to traffic.

I kept looking back toward the ridgeline to see where the fires were. We rounded a bend and the hills took away the view. My mind reeling, I knew what existed between the fire lines and where we stopped for gas. There were hundreds, perhaps thousands of homes. Scores of people whose lives and properties were in the fire's path would be destroyed. I felt very anxious and yet relieved at the same time. I realized the devastation the fire would leave in its wake and was thankful we had escaped!

The frenzied conversations in the car were of concerns for the people in the fire's path, astonishment at how quickly the fire leapt over the hills, and the devastation that it would leave in its wake. The children peppered us with questions about what would happen to the people.

We began to pray earnestly. Each of us took turns praying that the fire would be stopped. My wife prayed that the people would get out of its way. Each of our children prayed for the children who lived there. Our youngest prayed for the families' pets. I asked for rain and safety for the firefighters and policemen who responded. We all prayed that God would miraculously extinguish this fire.

Pastor Zach Bearss related his families' adventure July 1, 2012 to the Clearview Community Church in Bue-

> *Things that are never satisfied... fire, which never says enough!*
> *Proverbs 30:15b*

na Vista, Colorado. I visited the church that day. God had blessed me to be in Colorado to assemble this work. The trip had nearly been derailed due to the wildfires. After several phone calls and reassurance that the trip would be unaffected, I ventured to the Silver Cliff Ranch in Nathrop, Colorado, stewarded by Eric and Leta Dahlberg. A friend in the ministry, Pastor Jeff Johnson had made this adventure possible through his service on the board of Baptist Child and Family Services (BCFS). I had no idea when I asked friends to pray that BCFS had recently acquired and renovated the property in Nathrop. God is an amazing connector and I am especially grateful for BCFS and Silver Cliff Ranch's hospitality.

Only God can give us these connections and the picture of events in the world as it relates to our work and lives. He had already spoken to my heart about how the fires were representative of human trafficking in our world today. There is a raging fire of trafficking all around us but somehow it seems distant and someone else's problem to address.

The Colorado tinderbox conditions represent the world as it reflects a spiritual drought and the firestorm of criminal activity. All the conditions are right for the exploitation of people. The push and pull factors that help to enslave people create conditions beyond their control, often with no means of escape.

In the US, we have seen this as a distant problem that does not affect us. The whole notion that trafficking is somewhere else, and somebody else's issue continues to be problematic. As long as it is seen as "not in my backyard," we have no personal stake in human trafficking. The conditions of demand have brought trafficking to our backyards. My hope is that you will find in this book a "burning bush" experience. May you be compelled to personally see ways of responding to what may seem like distant issues of human trafficking that are actually raging very close, even touching your everyday life.

The suppression of a fire of this magnitude takes strategic planning. The hope of this book is that we are motivated to develop a more comprehensive and strategic response that includes Prevention, Intervention, Education, and Restoration.

It appears, up until now, we have come to the raging wildfire with only water pistols. It is time to call in the air units to deploy fire retardants and reinforcements on the ground. Moreover, we need to pray that God's "mighty hand will compel" an end to this atrocity. (Exodus 3:19)

This book is as much a calling as anything I have ever done in my 25 plus years of ministry. God specifically used Ezekiel chapters two and

> *Compelled by the Spirit... not knowing what will happen to me.*
> *Acts 20:22*

three in leading me to my missional call in human trafficking. The Denomination that I worked for adopted a resolution in 2006 condemning human trafficking. My ministry had been teaching the church to do the work of ministry in the criminal justice field. Naturally, human trafficking, being the fastest growing criminal enterprise in the world, qualified to be included in my work. In 2007, I began teaching the church about human trafficking.

During that same time, I stopped in my tracks as I read, Ezekiel 2:3:

He said: Son of Man, I am sending you to the Israelites, to a rebellious nation that has rebelled against me; they and their fathers have been in revolt against me to this very day. The people to whom I am sending you are obstinate and stubborn. Say to them, this is what the sovereign Lord says. And whether they listen or fail to listen – they are a rebellious house – they will know that a prophet has been among them.

I told God, "I am neither a prophet nor the child of a prophet, and I cannot see myself owning this scripture as a call." For two years God kept me camped in the Old Testament prophetic books, bringing me frequently back to Ezekiel. I am a bit of a slow learner at times and I am grateful for God's patience. He relentlessly persisted.

Then he said to me: 'Son of Man, go now to the house of Israel and speak my words to them. You are not being sent to the people of obscure speech and difficult language, but to the house of Israel—not to many peoples of obscure speech and difficult language, whose words you cannot understand. Surely if I had sent you to them, they would have listened to you. But the house of Israel is not willing to listen to you because they are not willing to listen to me, for the whole house of Israel is hardened and obstinate. But I will make you as unyielding and hardened as they are. I will make your forehead like the hardest stone, harder than flint. Do not be afraid of them or terrified by them, though they are a rebellious house."' Ezekiel 3:4

I found myself whining to God, "Great, I am called to be a missionary (I still could not see the prophet piece happening) in my home country or at least where they speak my language. The folks I speak to are already God's people and they will not want to hear what I have to say." Just the kind of call every believer would want. Nevertheless, I knew God persisted in showing me these Scriptures.

Ezekiel describes going as God had called him to his countrymen in exile and his awareness of the Spirit's presence. He says in verse 14, *"I went in bitterness and in the anger of my spirit, with the strong hand of the Lord upon me."* He came to where the exiles were living and records, *"I sat among them for seven days—overwhelmed."* I too had a sense of being overwhelmed not only by the call but also by the immensity of the issue of human trafficking.

The formation of this prophet calling still did not resonate in my spirit but I began to understand the call with the help of Ezekiel 3:16. *"At the end of seven days the word of the Lord came to me; Son of Man I have made you a watchman for the house of Israel; so hear the word I speak and give them warning from me."* Ezekiel took seven days; I think it took about seven months of praying to understand God's message to me.

God's word made it clear, I am not called as a prophet but as a watchman. It was an epiphany moment, complete with a rendition of the "Hallelujah Chorus." The watchman call made perfect sense to me. I had trained to be a police officer. I spent 12 years of my life as a 911-operator police and fire dispatcher. I had been a watchman, telling people of danger and helping them to get out of the way of trouble—like fires. I thought this calling would be easy and simple; after all no one was going to die (unlike my 911 days) based on whether I responded to it or not.

Almost immediately God took me to Ezekiel 3:18 to explain the seriousness of His call: *"When I say to a wicked man, 'You will surely die,' and you do not warn him or speak out to dissuade him of his evil ways in order to save his life, that wicked men will die for his sin, and I will hold you accountable for his blood. But if you do warn the wicked man and he does not turn from his wickedness or from his evil ways, he will die for his sin; but you will have saved yourself."*

Overwhelmed yet again, I had the Moses question, "Who am I?" Many other questions swirled in my head and heart. Dare I even speak of this watchman calling? Folks would think me a lunatic and perhaps by now you might agree. God knew I needed reassurance just as Ezekiel did repeatedly in his calling.

Ezekiel sensed God's Spirit (verse 22): *"The hand the Lord was upon me there . . . the glory of the Lord was standing there like the glory I had seen by the Kebar River and I fell facedown."* I knew that I needed the Holy Spirit's presence to be obedient as a watchman.

I came to know intimately the Lord's hand and presence. He led me to leave my full-time ministry position in May of 2010. Others in the ministry asked how I could leave a position of leadership in denominational life. My position would have been considered the pinnacle of a career with a good salary and great benefits.

To buffet the waves of doubt, God had me reading many books that challenged my thinking. Especially challenging was, "Don't Waste Your Life," by John Piper, which revealed my false sense of security in a job, title, position, or salary. I needed God's assurance when a major "interruption" occurred to responding to this call.

On July 11, 2010, I woke up in the middle of the night in severe pain. The hospital's doctor called it "a catastrophic surgical event" for which he gave me less than half a chance of living through the night. I spent the remainder of the year recovering. This is another book for another day. Suffice it to say, I cling daily and desperately to knowing His presence. I am greatly resolved to the call because of this sifting period.

Like Ezekiel, the Spirit's presence assures me when I speak to His people. God told him, *"I will open your mouth and you will say to them this is what the sovereign Lord says. Whoever will listen let him listen, and whoever will refuse to let him refuse; for they are a rebellious house."* (3:27)

As a watchman, I believe God is calling out to His church. He is reminding the church of the mis-

sion of Christ and why he said he came in Luke
4. My prayer is for the rebellious house to hear
that they are God's planned response and for
them to completely surrender heart, mind, soul,
and strength to His call. Will you join me in those
prayers?

Prayer should absolutely be our first response,
not a last resort. Prayer is the work and ministry
is the reward. If you plan to do anything because
of this book, start with prayer. Circle human trafficking in your mind with a bright red marker as
an issue you pray over regularly. Read "The Circle
Maker" by Mark Batterson to see what a difference encircling the issues of human trafficking
with prayer will make. See the other sections on
Prayerucation in the education chapter as well.

Why Now? Justice Now!

In 2009 I noticed a cosmic shift that is inexpli-
cable apart from God's action in drawing people
to His heart for the issues of justice in the world.
I have never seen, in my many years of ministry,
a clearer picture of God's activity and people responding whole-heartedly to His call. People of all
ages are responding but I see the current genera-

tion of young people (in their teens and 20's) on a spiritual quest for justice in their lifetime.

More articles, ministries, blogs, and "gloriously ruined ones" responding to God's call have happened since 2009 than I can enumerate here. The going was slow in the earlier years but the movement has reached a critical mass and is progressing rapidly. While many activities and organizations are disconnected from one another, there is a tangible collective forming.

A developing convergence of co-existent movements indicates that God's people are preparing to respond to Him concerning issues of justice. The abolitionists' movement focuses especially on human trafficking but much of the work must address the underlying causal factors through their efforts. Here are some examples of these converged movements. There is a movement for economic justice through the Acton University Poverty Cure[1] and Business as Mission.

Simultaneously, there is a movement for Christians to work in community development[2] and to do their work empowering individuals and com-

---

1   http://www.povertycure.org
2   Christian Community Development Association www.ccda.org

munities. "When Helping Hurts," by Corbett and Fikkert, instructs Christians on principles of indigenousness economic empowerment.[1] All of these are part of God's response to mitigate the circumstances that make people and communities vulnerable to traffickers. Another movement also exists in Community and Restorative Justice.[2] Some of these organizations work on restorative practices in local communities for empowering victims and addressing systemic issues.

Another example is the Passion Movement. Louie Giglio has been leading young people to experience God in the fullness of worship for a number of years.[3] Recently in Atlanta, Georgia, they focused on human trafficking and had a goal to raise $1 million dollars to assist in anti-trafficking efforts. By the end of the event, they had raised over $3 million. The funds went to various organizations in the fight against global trafficking as well as a house for the restoration of girls who had been exploited in the commercial sex industry in Georgia, Wellspring Living for Girls. They received national attention for this outpouring of response

---

1   www.whenhelpinghurts.org

2   www.restorativejusticenow.org

3   http://www.268generation.com/3.0/

in the news media and even the White House's Faith-based Initiatives director made public statements lauding the endeavors.

No discussion of human trafficking and justice issues in the world today would be complete without celebrating the more than ten years of work by the International Justice Mission (IJM).[1] This organization has created a great deal of momentum in the delivery of justice to individuals, communities, and the world. Gary Haugen has several books telling of their God ordained work to bring justice in the world.[2] He describes the beginnings of the International Justice Mission and their years of engagement successes and challenges. His challenge to the reader to have courage—the power to do the right thing even when it is scary and hard—resonates deeply with the original shape of our soul." (p103).

The work of IJM is significant in seeing God's heart for justice of the oppressed and enslaved. IJM has been a leader in a prayerful, holistic, and

---

1   www.IJM.org

2   "Good News About Injustice, Updated 10th Anniversary Edition: A Witness of Courage in a Hurting World," "Just Courage: God's Great Expedition for the Restless Christian" and "Terrify No More: Young Girls Held Captive and the Daring Undercover Operation to Win Their Freedom."

strategic response. They bring to bear an indige-nousness application of laws in countries rife with corruption and complicity in human exploitation. Their focus has been intentionally international and they represent God with excellence in their work. According to their website "IJM currently has ongoing operations in 15 cities in Cambodia, the Philippines, Thailand, India, Kenya, Rwanda, Uganda, Zambia, Bolivia and Guatemala, and has Casework Alliance Partnerships in Ecuador and Peru. IJM is headquartered in Washington, D.C., and has Partner Offices in Canada, Germany, the Netherlands, and the U.K."[1]

Gary Haugen, at Passion 2013 in Atlanta, gave a very enthusiastic presentation about what modern abolitionist need in order to engage the issues of trafficking. In brief, he gave five sets of words.

- Extravagant Compassion (Christ's love!)
- Moral Clarity (Found only in God's Word!)
- Sacrificial Courage (Facing evil with the bravery and courage of Christ in our hearts.)
- Persevering Hope (God is the God of Justice!)

---

1 www.ijm.org

- Refreshing Joy (Oxygen for doing hard things with never failing commitment.)

He began with the exhortation that Human Trafficking will end when God's "A" team has these five things in their hearts! I would add personal ownership to the list. Christ calls each of us to make a personal decision about Him. Just as we must decide about our salvation—we must each decide to do our part! Movements take commitment beyond just lip service to the problem; they take a change in our own behavior.

A movement of morality that is not necessarily based on Christian principles is also worth noting. Nicholas Kristoff and Sheryl WuDunn have started a movement which highlights the plight of girls in the global arena and viable solutions to reduce their victimization. This movement is helping to re-frame the global dialogue on women and girls.[1]

The movements listed above are global and local in their responses. Many other organizations exist that are addressing man's inhumanity to man in trafficking. Some are intentional about their Christian calling to the issues while others

---

1   Their book is called, "Half the Sky." Also see the TED Talk video, "Our Century's Greatest Injustice" http://www.ted.com/talks/lang/eng/sheryl_wudunn_our_century_s_greatest_injustice.html

have faith as only a piece of their response but faith is not their "why."[1] The movements are representative of how God is passionately calling His people to the justice work of Jesus. In Luke 4:18 Jesus reads from Isaiah 61: *The Spirit of the Lord is on me, because he has anointed me to proclaim good news to the poor. He has sent me to proclaim freedom for the prisoners and recovery of sight for the blind, to set the oppressed free, to proclaim the year of the Lord's favor.*

This is why we, who call ourselves Christians, respond to the injustices we see in the world. This is our true "why" when we respond to the burning bush experience. God is seeing,

> *He has showed you, O man, what is good. And what does the Lord require of you? To act justly and to love mercy and to walk humbly with your God.*
> *Micah 6:8*

hearing, compassionately responding, and sending us just like Jesus. Jesus came to show us God's heart for justice.

---

1   A website that serves as a virtual clearinghouse of books, websites, media, and resource to find many faith-based organizations and others (www.aheartforjustice.com).

Listen to the original burning bush experience: *Now Moses was tending the flock of Jethro his father-in-law, the priest of Midian, and he led the flock to the far side of the desert and came to Horeb, the mountain of God. There the angel of the Lord appeared to him in flames of fire from within the bush. Moses saw that though the bush was on fire it did not burn up. So Moses thought, "I will go over and see this strange site—why the bush does not burn up."* (Exodus 3:1–3)

God's all consuming presence in the midst of a burning bush appears to Moses. Fire in a bush and it does not burn up, no doubt was compelling. Moses was drawn to this unusual sight. He had been about his everyday business and suddenly is confronted with an unusual experience. He had a choice to make about responding to the burning bush before him. God drew Moses there to give attention to an issue of His concern, slavery. The stories of the Egyptians and their enslavement of the Israelites were not news to Moses. He had lived the story since birth. His story was inextricably linked to God's assignment for him.

Desperation brought the Israelites into the clutches of the Egyptians. The famine was so severe the Israelites went in search of food sources. They sold all of their personal items, all their cattle, everything they had, even their very lives to get access to food. I encourage you to read the full story in Genesis 37–47. It will be important to understand the desperation for food in later chapters that discuss the present factors contributing to the global situations of slavery.

The Moses story resonates with many of the people I have talked to over the last five years as I have taught on human trafficking. Mike and Norma Mullican are one example of this burning bush experience. They were retiring from their life's work and had a plan in place about how they would spend their retirement. They were going about their everyday business of a wedding chapel and catering company.

Norma and her daughter Missy had written a children's book ("A Collection of Squirrel Tales"). They were looking for an opportunity to support the work of a "worthwhile" non-profit. Norma said in an interview, "We started exploring and learned of an organization working with children who had been trafficked into the sex industry in Cambodia. We learned they had safe homes there and we wanted the money to go to help there."

She related that this was their burning bush experience of God drawing them in and showing them more. They learned about sexual exploitation of children in the United States, in their state, and in their own community. "We started seeing the issue was all around us. After six months of praying, God solidified it in our hearts that He was calling us to respond very specifically by developing a safe home in our community," Norma recounted.

During those six months of prayer and discernment, Norma said, "We realized it is really about God. Our response is God using ordinary people no matter their age or background to do His work."

We will visit more with the Mullican's story in the chapter on restoration of victims. First, we need to explore more about what God was telling Moses at the burning bush.

"The Lord said, "I have indeed seen the misery of my people in Egypt. I have heard them crying out because of their slave drivers, and I am concerned about their suffering. So I have come down to rescue them from the hand of the Egyptians and to bring them out of the land into a good and spacious land..." (Exodus 3:7–8)

God says three things to Moses in this passage. "I have seen, I have heard, I am concerned." He added one more item in verse 10, "I am sending you." God was compassionately responding to the misery, the cries of the people and he was demonstrating his concern by sending Moses to free them from their slave drivers.

Moses responds immediately to God's assignment with a series of questions and excuses. We should not fault Moses for his response over being sent to Pharaoh. Consider Moses' situation. Remember he had been raised in Pharaoh's household. He was an Israelite. He had many reasons why he should not go. None of his excuses were beyond God's recognition. In reality, by God's design Moses was the perfect person to take up this challenge before Pharaoh.

God's call for Moses also came with help from the Israelite elders. In verse 16, God assures help to Moses. *"Go, assemble the elders of Israel and say to them, The Lord the God of your fathers—the God of Abraham, Isaac and Jacob – appeared to me and said: I have watched over you and have seen what has been done to you in Egypt and I have promised to bring it up out of misery of Egypt into the land... flowing with milk and honey."*

In response to what Moses told the elders, they believed that the God of the Hebrews had a mission for them. *"Let us take a three-day journey into the desert to offer sacrifices to the Lord our God."* (v18)

God was with them in the desert and was guiding their response. He assured them that He would be with them saying, *"But I know that the king of Egypt will not let you go unless some mighty hand compels him. So I will stretch out my hand, and strike the Egyptians with all the wonders that I will perform among them. After that, he will let you go."* (19-20)

The scope of human trafficking for most people is overwhelming. For several years, I taught about human trafficking with the big picture. I would cite several studies that showed there are 27 million slaves around the world today. Soodalter the historian says there are "more people enslaved around the world than in any other time even during the 350 years of trans-Atlantic slave trade." The shock and awe overwhelmed them.

People would walk away from my presentations as if they had been drinking from a fire hose. The looks on their faces told me they were stunned and paralyzed by information overload.

Afterwards they would ask, "What do I do? What can one person do?"

Sometimes I would hear the Moses questions. "Who am I?" or "Who will listen to me?" Many questions centered on "What should I do?"

After praying about the responses, I asked God to show me how to help people understand the issues better and how they could respond. God indicated that to communicate the "why" of responding to human trafficking was initially more important than the "what" they were to do.

I realized that the "why" message of today is the exact same thing that God told Moses at the burning bush. He is seeing what is happening, he is hearing the cries of the children, and he is compassionately responding. God sent Moses to tell the elders and they would respond with him. He is doing the same today. God is raising up responses in the Christian church.

God did not have a "Plan B" to free the slaves from the Egyptians. Moses and the elders were His plan. I have concluded that God does not have a "Plan B" to free the slaves in our world today. As God has been revealing to His people around the world the atrocities of human trafficking, He is also calling people through "burning bush" experiences to respond.

There is no way that I could know each person's part of God's response equation. Only God can tell them what to do. It was the beginning point for me to package the information in a way that people could grasp a possible trajectory for their personal response. They could begin assessing their calling personally.

I also saw the need for a more focused and simple message about the "what" to do. God showed me four main components of response were imbedded in the trainings I had been providing: prevention, intervention, education, and restoration. From these four areas, participants can begin to assess how God might be leading the "what" of their response.

Months after one particular presentation I had woman call me to say thanks for all of the information. She said, "But now I am waking up at night with the cries of children in my dreams." My response to her—you must be hearing what God hears, the cries of the children who are enslaved around the world. We talked through what that might look like for her in her local community.

She was set in a direction to explore God's specific calling.

It does not surprise me that people are hearing in their dreams the children crying out for rescue. God is waking them up to the realities. It is well documented in many publications and reports on human trafficking from organizations like Free the Slaves that half (50%) of all the victims of trafficking in the world our children.[1](See the Appendix for more informational resources).

After Moses' three days in the desert, there is no indication in the Scripture that Moses continued tending sheep. He was now tending to the slaves in Egypt as their shepherd. He left his work and ordinary way of life to do what God called him to do.

Since 2007, I have met a number of "burning bush" people called by God to respond to the issues of trafficking. Some have used their professions as a platform that God alone could have designed and others have actually left their jobs. Just like me.

One of those who left her corporate position is Deena Graves. She worked in the high-tech industry in business communications. I expect she

---

1   http://www.freetheslaves.net

would say she was at the top of her game. She had climbed the corporate ladder and was doing well in her career, making a very comfortable salary.

Deena's burning bush experience came in a presentation at her church by a ministry that was working in Cambodia with victims of trafficking. They told of the little girls who were sold into the brothels. A fellow church member, a police officer in Dallas, was in conversation with Deena about this presentation. She remarked about how horrible that this happened in Cambodia. Furthermore, she was glad this did not happen in the United States. He was quick to correct her, "No, this happens right here on the streets that I work every day."

She was stunned. Many sleepless nights and much prayer followed this revelation. The thought of this happening in the United States derailed Deena's everyday life. God began showing her something that was unexpected. Her routine of attending a church event brought trafficking in her face as a "burning bush" moment. She began studying the issue in the United States and started asking many questions looking at available documents to disprove this. She soon realized that American children were being bought and sold in the sex industry in the very community where her church was located.

After much prayer and consideration with her family, small group, and Pastor, Deena left her corporate job. She began a nonprofit organization to work with high risk and at-risk youth through prevention as well as to provide restorative housing for girls coming out of the sex industry.[1] We will visit more of Deena's story in later chapters concerning prevention and restoration.

God proved to me you are never too young to become an abolitionist. Benjamin Sherman at age eight responded to what he had learned about human trafficking at church by writing a story about how to help the children in Cambodia.[2]

Larry Megason's story demonstrates another avenue God uses to open His people to the work He has for them. His burning bush experience came during a mission to trip to Haiti in 2011 after a massive earthquake devastated a significant portion of the island. Here is a glimpse of his experience there.

---

1   Traffick911 www.traffick911.org
2   Learn more about "Gregory's Paper Airplane" at the website: http://gregoryspaperairplane.com

I had the privilege of making my first trip to this amazing little country. Poverty has always dominated the landscape. Devastation surrounded us. My primary focus in traveling to Haiti had been to provide clothing, hygiene items, and other resources to orphans. Our other goals were to assist in the development of sustainable business models including tilapia farms, chicken coops, gardens, bakeries, water wells, and more.

I visited with a pastor in the Tabarre Province NE of Port au Prince surveying a two acre piece of property where we were to build an orphanage and dig a well for clean water. We drove onto the land, we noticed a man using his machete to cut down banana trees. We called him over to ask about his activities. He responded, "The owner told me to do this."

The pastor I was traveling with calmly replied, "I'm the owner."

The man began to argue, and then was joined by another man with a machete, then a third, and a fourth. Feeling the tension rising, the pastor and I plotted our retreat when a fifth man joined the group. He had no machete.

The last man brought with him a seven-year-old Haitian girl. I thought nothing of it until he addressed me face-to-face, "Would you like to buy her?"

I could not believe his question and I said, "What?"

He again asked me, "Would you like to buy her? She will do good things for you. $9."

I immediately said, "No!"

The Pastor and I moved to the van and quickly left. I can still see her bright, beautiful, fearful eyes as I watched her in my rearview mirror through my own tears. During our visit, I had a significant epiphany. I had never been offered to "buy" a human before.

Selling this child seemed so easy for this man. I knew people were very hungry, but I could not fathom selling a child much less selling one for sexual services. While I was there, I visited many tent cities and saw the excruciating hardships of life in this otherwise beautiful place.

My heart was broken over these experiences. Above the local, national, and global struggles I witnessed in my life, this one encounter changed everything. I had a divine encounter, an epiphany. I have served in vocational ministry most of my adult life, and chosen early in life to be mission minded, even mission driven. Being in Haiti was a normal missional endeavor to me. What God did in my life in Haiti was anything but normal.

When I returned from Haiti my service in the local church was no longer "enough." I could not be just another missional man. For me, that was unacceptable. God "ruined" me forever returning to life, as I once knew it. I began researching the buying and selling of humans in Haiti. I found this was a global phenomenon. But when I researched the issue in the United States my heart melted within me. How could I have missed this horrific evil in my own country? How did I not know modern slavery of all kinds had surpassed even what our country experienced during the vile time of the Atlantic African slave trade?

I realized modern slavery is even more sinister and far-reaching than I imagined. What we could plainly see and experience openly with early American slavery is now hidden, driven from view in American culture. My heart was broken for my country.

As much as I wanted to stand tall and scream loudly at the darkness hoping to push it back, I knew I did not possess the skills or the singular courage to significantly influence this tsunami of evil. Nevertheless, I did raise my voice. I cried out to my heavenly Father to break my heart even more; to see the enslaved through His eyes, His heart, and His compassion. He reminded me that I am the lineage of Levi, the worship warrior. He took my missional heart and infused it with a vision. It is a God-sized vision. For me, the vision is birthed in the form of a non-profit "Restore A Voice."

Restore A Voice (RAV) began as the people God gathered around the vision; artists, entrepreneurs, strategists, abolitionists, and more. He was developing a skilled leadership team infusing them with a vision that would see the darkness pushed back. He provided supporters whose hearts were broken over the enslavement of children, young women, and men. These supporters catapulted Restore A Voice forward. We traveled across America to see who was providing an answer. We learned sitting at the feet of those who had gone before us. Along the journey, we collaborated with exceptional grassroots organizations like Allies Against Slavery in Austin, Texas. Our collective voices helped raise awareness and educate thousands. We were doing more than enlightening them. The spark lit a fire for a collaborative raised voice.[1]

---

1   Read more of Larry's story in the Intervention section.

Cosmic Shift

The cosmic shift of 2009, which I mentioned earlier, was in God's response to the issues of trafficking especially with His people in the United States. Norma and Deena are two of a larger group who also had the "burning bush" experience. I have begun fondly referring to them as the "gloriously ruined ones." Most of the group identified early 2009 as when we were put on this journey individually. It was in 2010 that God began to connect us. When we met, we discovered God's amazing activity with all of us.

God's people must begin with a response of prayer. Gathering others from the church, like the elders in the story of Moses. A season of prayer or a period, perhaps three days, to seek God's face and to ask him what he would have them to do. No initial response to human trafficking by the church of Jesus Christ would be appropriate without prayer and fasting

> *So God created man in his own image, in the image of God he created him; male and female he created them.*
> *Genesis 1:27*

to seek God. He is the one who has to show you your gifts, skills, talents, and abilities as well as how He has created your life story as a piece of the response.

Stewardship of Humanity

God cares for His creation. He is a compassionate steward and all of us are of value in his sight. While we are all individuals, we are a part of the whole of humanity. God teaches us about His stewardship of humanity through Jesus Christ. He sent Christ to demonstrate His love and stewardship.

> *For God so loved the world that he gave his one and only Son, that whoever believes in him shall not perish but have eternal life. For God did not send his Son into the world to condemn the world, but to save the world through him.*
> *John 3:16*

He meant what He said. In His eyes, every human being is of value. If that were not so then we would need to be worried about our own salvation. The reality is each of us is valued in God's sight and we have equal access to Him through faith in Jesus Christ.

The body of Christ's followers is described similarly in1 Corinthians 12:12: *"The body is a unit, though it is made up of many parts; and though all its parts are many, they form one body. So it is with Christ."* We must grapple with the fact we are all part of the larger humanity and we have responsibilities to each other by God's design. If one part of our body is infected by a cancerous growth, it affects the whole body. Humanity is infected by criminal enterprise and horrific cancerous oppression.

In medical terms, we have a public health issue. In order for all of humanity to be a healthy organism, we need to apply radical preventative measures (addressing the causal factors) plus certain and effective interventions to eradicate the problem. Victims affected by this cancer will also need intensive rehabilitative treatment.

> *There is neither Jew nor Greek, slave nor free, male nor female, for all are one in Christ Jesus.*
> *Galatians 3:28*

Christ's mission and ministry bring the stewardship of humanity to the church's doorstep. We cannot ignore the existence of the cancer or not respond to it. Ignoring cancer does not make it go away. We see this in Scripture as it refers to the church body. 1 Corinthians 12:26-27: *"If one part suffers, every part suffers with it; if one part is honored, every part rejoices with it. Now you are the body of Christ, and each one of you is a part of it."*

The value of humanity is decreasing globally. In the days of the Trans-Atlantic slave trade the average cost of a slave in those days was a sizeable sum nearing $40,000.00 in today's economy.[1] Today it is reported that the average cost of a slave around the world is less than $90.00.[2] The rental of a slave by the minute or portions of an hour is in some countries only a few dollars. Men, women, boys, and girls created in the image of God do not come with price tags.

Some of the victims of human trafficking include believers in Jesus Christ. For whatever reason and by whatever means they got there—we may never know. What we do know is that a part of the body of Christ is enslaved and it affects the whole body. Just as any member of humanity that is enslaved affects the whole of humanity.

---

1 http://www.slavevoyages.org/tast/index.faces
2 http://www.freetheslaves.net

In the United States, the Declaration of Independence declares these concepts: "We hold these truths to be self-evident, that all men are created equal, that they are endowed by their Creator with certain unalienable Rights, that among these are Life, Liberty and the pursuit of Happiness." This document reflects God's creative oversight and stewardship of all human beings.

Curiously, this document was written during a time of slavery and in the midst of an abolitionist movement in England. The duplicitous thinking of the world at that time erroneously allowed for both the freedom of one part of humanity and the enslavement of another. Since then some wrong thinking has been addressed. Contrary to many people's thinking slavery in the US did not end with the Emancipation Proclamation. Unfortunately, it served to send slavery underground and allow it to flourish as a new kind of oppression of peoples. I would encourage you to visit The Freedom Center in Cincinnati, Ohio, for

> *Live as free men, but do not use your freedom as a cover-up for evil; live as servants of God.*
> *1 Peter 2:16*

more information.[1] You will see actual slave quarters, documents, and artifacts describing the conditions of slavery over the centuries, the network of the Underground Railroad, and stories including modern day slavery.

We enjoy many freedoms in the United States; unfortunately, those freedoms can be used to allow for the subjugation of others. We must not give up on the principles of freedom that our Creator designed for humanity.

Our freedom in Christ can be an instrument for good in changing the dynamics of the present reality of slavery in our world today. We must take freedom seriously and approach human trafficking with God's practices of stewardship and great love for humanity.

Two Scriptures that greatly influenced my work in human trafficking are Proverbs 24:11 and 12. *"Rescue those being led away to death; hold back those staggering towards slaughter."* This is a clarion call for a watchman. God is calling his body to respond. Typically, I use verse 12 to wrap up my presentations to churches as a challenge to the body. *"If you say, 'But we knew nothing about this,' does not he who weighs the heart perceive it?*

---

1   http://www.freedomcenter.org/

Does not he who guards your life know it? Will he not repay everyone according to what they have done?"

Perhaps William Wilberforce was influenced by this verse as well. He spent his entire political career working on abolishing the slave trade. His work effected great changes in England and the world beyond. He influenced President Lincoln's work to end the slave trade in the United States. Who will the present abolitionists' movement influence in future generations?

Stewardship of the Children

Every child comes marked, stamped, and tattooed with the indelible, albeit invisible, image of God. No matter what color the skin, eyes, or hair, that child is an image bearer. Whether they are born in Burma or Boston, Nigeria or New York, it does not matter. They are all God's creation. They do not come with price tags, but rather as priceless.

The valuing of children in the whole of humanity holds a special place in Christ's ministry. He demonstrated his care and value for them many times. Parents saw how Christ's blessings would be important for their children. People brought their babies to Jesus to have Him touch them as a symbol of blessing.

The disciples discouraged interruption because they saw this as bothering Jesus with unimportant matters. But Jesus called the children to him and said, *'Let the little children come to me, and do not hinder them, for the kingdom of God belongs to such as these.'* (Luke 18:16)

> *Things that cause people to sin are bound to come, but woe to that person through whom they come. It would be better for him to be thrown into the sea with a millstone tied around his neck than for him to cause one of these little ones to sin.*
> Luke 17:1–2

Christ's availability for the children demonstrated His stewardship over them and their value to him.

In Matthew 11:25 *"... Jesus said, "I praise you, Father, Lord of heaven and earth, because you have hidden these things from the wise and learned, and revealed them to little children. Yes, Father for this was your good pleasure."* Christ was using the faith of children to teach others about Himself and the Kingdom of God.

Speaking to His disciples, Jesus spoke of God's value of children in Mark 9:36, *"He took a little child and had him stand among them. Taking him in his arms, he said to them, 'Whoever welcomes one of these little children in my name welcomes me; and whoever welcomes me does not welcome me but the one who sent me.'"*

Christ knew that children trusted and believed readily in Him. The children knew He valued them and believing was a very natural simple response. In Luke 18: 17 Jesus says, *"I tell you the truth, anyone who will not receive the kingdom of God like a little child will never enter it."* We must emulate Christ's acceptance and love for children in our stewardship.

God creates families on purpose. The stewardship of children is a responsibility first to parents as the Scripture gives clear instructions to teach them about the Lord as referenced in Deuteronomy 4:9, 6:7, and 11:9. The church has a natural role in teaching parents how to teach their children as well as providing additional teaching opportunities through church activities. The church can play a vital role in single parent families in an extended family role.

The church must play an active role in teaching parents about mitigating the current culture's influence on their children. Churches can take the opportunities available to teach about sexual abuse and how abuse creates a trajectory of children to exploitation. They can teach children to resist people who try to harm them. The church can become the protector of the future generations as it stewards the children under their care.

Valuable resources and curriculums that I recommend to churches and parents are available from Darkness to Light[1] and Purehope.[2] Other materials exist and are included in the prevention section and in the appendices.

The church can also play a major role in caring for orphans in our society. James 1:27 tells us to look after orphans and widows. In our current US culture, our modern-day widows are single mothers. In census data for the United States, the number of never married single mothers and previously married single mothers are about equal. This means that large portions of children in our society are being raised in single parent households.

---

1   www.d2l.org

2   www.Purehope.net

Addressing the causal factors for this phenomenon in our society would be advantageous as well in the prevention of the exponential perpetuation of these issues. Helping this generation to have a moral compass about sexuality and child rearing is a task squarely in line with the church's mission of stewardship.

According to Darkness to Light, an education and prevention organization, it is highly likely that you know a child who has been or is being abused. The statistics of sexual abuse in the United States are staggering.

- Experts estimate that 1 in 4 girls and 1 in 6 boys are sexually abused before their 18th birthdays. This means that in any classroom or neighborhood full of children, there are children who are silently bearing the burden of sexual abuse.
- 1 in 5 children are sexually solicited while on the Internet. (A growing percentage through social media such as Facebook.)
- Nearly 70% of all reported sexual assaults (including assaults on adults) occur to children ages 17 and under.
- The median age for reported sexual abuse is nine-years-old.

- Approximately 20% of the victims of sexual abuse are under age eight.
- 50% of all victims of forcible sodomy, sexual assault with an object, and forcible fondling are under age twelve.
- Most child victims never report the abuse. (Threats and shaming are used.)
- Sexually abused children who keep it a secret or who "tell" and are not believed are at greater risk than the general population for psychological, emotional, social, and physical problems, often lasting into adulthood.
- It is also likely that you know an abuser. The greatest risk to children does not come from strangers but from friends and family.
- 30-40% of children are abused by family members.
- As many as 60% are abused by people the family trusts–abusers frequently try to form a trusting relationship with parents.
- Nearly 40% are abused by older or larger children (sometimes siblings).
- People who abuse children look and act just like everyone else. In fact, they often

go out of their way to appear trustworthy to gain access to children.

- Those who sexually abuse children are drawn to settings where they can gain easy access to children, such as sports leagues, faith centers, clubs, and schools.

Darkness to Light also demonstrates the immediate and long-term consequences to children and to our society.[1]

- 70-80% of sexual abuse survivors report excessive drug and alcohol use.
- One study showed that among male survivors, 50% have suicidal thoughts and more than 20% attempt suicide.
- Young girls who are sexually abused are more likely to develop eating disorders as adolescents.
- More than 60% of teen first pregnancies are preceded by experiences of molestation, rape, or attempted rape. The average age of the offenders is 27-years-old.
- Approximately 40% of sex offenders report sexual abuse as children.

---

1   www.d2l.org/site/c.4dICIJOkGcISE/b.6178667/
k.62D3/Step_1_Learn_the_Facts.htm

- Both males and females who have been sexually abused are more likely to engage in prostitution. (Nearly 80% of adult women in the sex industry say that they began as a teenager.)
- Approximately 70% of sexual offenders of children have between one and nine victims; 20-25% have 10 to 40 victims.
- Serial child molesters may have as many as 400 victims in their lifetimes.

This is a public health issue. If we had a disease or medical issue in the US that we knew would infect 25% of our girls and approximately 17% of our boys, what would we be doing differently? Would there not be an outcry from the public to eradicate the cause, vaccinate our children, increase prevention efforts, treatment protocols, and disease reduction efforts?

There is a national government plan called "Project Safe Childhood."[1] The scope of this project has focused at the prosecutorial and law enforcement aspects with little strength in the grassroots community level. Cases of sexual abuse like the Sandusky case at Penn State University are usu-

---

1   www.projectsafechildhood.gov

ally the only time media attention is given to child sexual abuse. The initiative has little impact on societal change. An organization that has responded to this issue is Stop it Now.[1]

In order to fulfill our call to be stewards of children, we must create a climate to change society. A full media campaign that rivals the "Smokey the Bear" or the "Susan G. Komen, Race for the Cure," breast cancer campaign would be a great start. The "Pink Ribbon" campaign is very effective and represents 12.5% of women in the United States compared to 25% of girls who will be sexually abused before their 18th birthday. The church can help by being a voice for the voiceless. There would be great strength in a church-based educational program and prevention effort in our local communities. These will be discussed in the prevention and education chapters ahead.

Stewardship in the Global Arena

Around the world the issues affecting children are staggering. Poverty, famine, starvation, polluted water, HIV/AIDS, and war are a few of the key issues. Medical problems created by easily addressed issues kill millions of children every

---

1 www.stopitnow.org

year. According to the World Health Organization, "a child dies every 15 seconds from water-related diseases" (WHO, 2004). Children in the midst of crises are exceptionally vulnerable to exploitation and trafficking. According to UNICEF's 2008 report, there is "an estimated 925 million hungry people in the world, 13.1 percent, or almost 1 in 7 people are hungry." Additionally, "poor nutrition plays a role in at least half of the 7.6 million child deaths each year."[1]

The number of orphans in the world contributes to the problem for children according to the United Nations. Every 60 seconds a woman dies of complications related to pregnancy or childbirth in sub-Saharan Africa, one of every 100 live births results in the mother's death. This is a representation of the gravity of the problem that there are whole villages where children are caring for children. "The Hole in our Gospel," by Richard Stearns, would be an excellent resource to gain more understanding of the global issues that children face and the solutions approach that World Vision has taken to address in various countries throughout the world.

---

1   http://www.worldhunger.org

What does it look like to be a steward of children in these desperate conditions? Kimberly L. Smith is President and co-founder of Make Way Partners (MWP).[1] She and her husband Milton live in Sylacauga, Alabama. They served as missionaries in the Iberian Peninsula when they first discovered human trafficking in 2002. They found children trafficked through an orphanage and it changed their lives. They spent the next two years learning all they could about human trafficking. Their research came from the streets, sewers, desert, and jungle as well as books and government reports, but most importantly, from spending time with victims of trafficking and those most vulnerable.

One of God's specifically called stewards of children, Kimberly divides her time between MWP's locations around the world, writing, and speaking in the US. She is a devoted wife, mother, and grandmother. She loves to read, write, and enjoys the out of doors with Milton and their dogs. An ordinary woman used for extraordinary purposes by God. Kimberly has written the story of God's work through her in "Passport Through

---

1   www.makewaypartners.org

Darkness," which I highly recommend.[1] Kimberly's blogs about what God is actively doing in and through their ministry. She is compelled and called to write about the children. "It seemed that, aside from working to save helpless children myself, the most important thing I could do with my life was to help other people also know God's heart–particularly for orphans—and find their personal steps to the music of His heart."

Make Way Partners cares for over 1,000 orphans in three locations in Sudan, including a war-ravaged location in the Nuba mountains. Their facilities are all indigenously managed, but supported and funded from primarily US sources. The needs are much greater than this facility can hold. Turning away children back to the bush areas is heart breaking for the ministry and it grieves her and her indigenousness staff who knows the dangers first hand. They are constantly expanding and seeking new partners who will help them with child sponsorship and building projects.

Other Options

Adoption is another potential way that churches can play an active role in being stewards of chil-

---

1   Ibid.

dren. Many ministries work with couples to make adoption possible. Loving and caring for children in the name of Christ should mean opening our hearts, our homes, and our churches as a community of caring. The needs are both in the US and International context. These become "our children" when we know that God is calling us to be stewards of His little image bearers.[1]

Child sponsorship is another avenue of providing stewardship of children and reducing their vulnerabilities to trafficking. Make Way Partners has sponsorship options as well as large organizations such as World Vision and Compassion International. Some small organizations exist that strive to work in communities that are rife with poverty and hunger to build the capacity of the families to care for their children and orphans in their communities. They provide community development options for empowering small farms and businesses as well as education. It is important to look for organizations with good financial accountability and also focus on developing indigenousness leaders and solutions. More informa-

---

1   See the organization http://www.christianallianceforrorphans.org for more information on how to engage on adoption issues.

tion will be in a later chapter about education and restoration.

The children are the future. The church is uniquely positioned to make a difference in the lives of children in our communities and in our world. We can respond and we must no longer shirk our responsibility as stewards of the children.

Owning our Part

Most people I talk to have not come to the realization that they contribute to trafficking personally. My presentations normally begin with a few short facts about human trafficking in the economics of globalization of products, goods, and services. I ask a series of questions, "Where was your shirt made? Do you know if the hands that produced your clothing were those of someone enslaved?" Then I ask about what they have eaten this week such as fruits, vegetables, or chocolate and the hands that were involved in those producing those foods.

These become epiphany moments as to how our global markets and consumerism has fueled the exploitation of workers and enslaved many people around the world. One book that I highly recommend to discover more and to learn Biblical principles concerning these issues is "Everyday Justice" by Julie Clawson.[1] She discusses how our "everyday choices support systems of injustice that oppress our neighbors..." and endeavors to equip readers in "discovering practical everyday ways we can seek justice ..."

There is an interactive, award winning website[2] I recommend for those who want to explore their contribution to the problem. This site will help you explore your household's slavery footprint. However, this exercise falls short when it comes to discussing the relevant contributions that we make to the proliferation of the sex industry which fuels sex trafficking both locally and globally.

Most people can easily grasp how they contribute to the labor trafficking issues and how they can make personal changes in their buying habits to minimize their footprints in labor trafficking. Being good stewards is a cornerstone of the Christian faith and should lead us to think deeply about

---

1   http://www.everydayjustice.net
2   http://www.slaveryfootprint.org

our stewardship of what we buy. I will talk more about slave free merchandise in future chapters.

The difficulty comes when the discussion turns to our personal contributions to sex trafficking both locally and globally. Half of all victims of trafficking are in the commercial sex industry. Women and children represent about 80% of these victims. The slaveryfootprint.org website stops short of addressing these issues.

Millions of women, girls, and boys are forced to provide sex for sale by methods of force, fraud, or coercion in global sex tourism. The demand for sexual services in the

Now listen, you rich people, weep and wail because of the misery that is coming upon you. Your wealth has rotted, and moths have eaten your clothes. Your gold and silver are corroded. Their corrosion will testify against you and eat your flesh like fire. You have hoarded wealth in the last days. Look! The wages you failed to pay the workmen who mowed your fields are crying out against you. The cries of the harvesters have reached the ears of the Lord Almighty. You have lived on earth in luxury and self-indulgence. You have fattened yourselves in the day of slaughter. You have condemned and murdered innocent men, who were not opposing you. Jms 5:1-6 world is a part of a phenomenon of sexual perversity, pederasty, pedophilia, pornography, and prostitution. This is a part of the global pandemic of HIV/AIDS. There is a significant amount of research on these medical aspects, which are truly a public health crisis.[1]

The proliferation of this demand is fueled by silence about sexual abuse and cultural normalization of engagement of children in sexual behaviors. Children are hyper-sexualized by media, music, clothing, and pornography. The greatest demand in the porn industry is for children in pornography. The sadistic rape and torture of children videoed and placed on the Internet is growing exponentially.

The other part of the equation is in what you consume or turn a blind eye to through the music, movies, and clothing choices/sexualized fashion, and tolerance of pornography on the web. There are other venues where commodification of sex for "sale" is tolerated. Ladies, are you complicit by what you wear or buy? This aspect of the sex industry has been infiltrating our society for a long time but that does not mean we should be silent against it. The targeted audience is our children.

---

1   See research at: http://www.iom.edu.

Even in their preschool years, they are being hyper-sexualized by all of these exposure points.

It is not enough to say, "I do not buy sexualized merchandise." Moreover, do you speak up against it as a steady diet in our culture? If you think it is not affecting you, I dare you to consider how many sexualized images are bombarding you every day from the news to the television shows you watch. One group of media specialists and successful women has taken on this challenge in a documentary called "Miss Representation." Consider hosting a watch party event and a discussion group.

There are three factors to consider in any discussion about these issues.

Point 1: Abuse and the silence that surrounds it are like a cancer in the United States. It is there; we know it is there. Nevertheless, we continue to find victims who did not or could not speak up and perpetrators are not held accountable for whatever reason. Look at cases like Penn State in the news for a sexual abuse scandal in 2012. It is estimated in the United States alone that eighty percent (80%) of the victims of commercial sexual exploitation have been abused as children.[1] The

---

1   www.sharedhope.org

proliferation of this demand for sex with children is fueled by silence about sexual abuse.

Point 2: The demand is great. The porn industry is profiting off the abuse of children in pornography and the demand is growing. Some people who view images of porn become desensitized to the images and begin to act out in real life what they have viewed. This includes younger people who are engaged with pornographic images by accident or by intention of their own curiosity or the exposure by a peer or predator.[1]

Point 3: Addresses the layer of the cultural normalization of engagement of children in sexual behaviors. Children are hyper-sexualized by media, music, clothing, and pornography. Recent cases citing children in beauty contests being dressed as "hookers" from the movie Pretty Woman document the challenges girls face in this culture.[2]

Hyper-sexualization that includes a stripper pole kit marketed for preschoolers should help to

1   For more information see: www.socialcostsofpornography.org/ and www.internetsafety101.org/101_video_clips.htm. These sites include studies about the medical and psychological effects of porn that elaborate on the prevalence and problems for children.

2   http://www.washingtonpost.com/blogs/celebritology/post/toddlers-and-tiaras-contestant-dresses-as-pretty-woman-prostitute/2011/09/07/gIQAErb78J_blog.html

illuminate the fact that children are being bombarded with sexual messages and groomed for engagement very early.[1] One professor of education Diane Levin has written about this phenomenon and has tips for parents on addressing this issue in her book "So Sexy So Soon."[2]

What does all of this have to do with our responsibility concerning sex trafficking?

Think about these questions:

- When was the last time you recognized the issue in everyday life as it comes across your eyes and ears?
- How have you addressed your personal consumption of music, movies, and clothing choices/sexualized fashion, tolerance of pornography on the web or in other venues where commodification of sex for "sale" is tolerated?
- Are you complicit by those choices or have you been silent about this issue?
- What proactive steps have you taken to make a difference in what is being offered to society?

---

1   Here is a series of stories from ABC news demonstrating the targeting of young girls for sexualized products: http://abcnews.go.com/2020/video/young-sexy-15031065.

2   http://dianeelevin.com/sosexysosoon/

The Culture of "Knuckleheads"

Buying sex with children under 18 should not be tolerated or minimized. We should expect the condemnation of the practice by government officials.

In April, 2012 a dozen Secret Service officials were investigated for misconduct, excessive drinking, and cavorting with prostitutes, ahead of President Obama's trip to Cartagena, Colombia. The White House held a press conference April 24th. "The actions of the knuckleheads accused of misconduct in the Secret Service scandal should not diminish the importance of the agency's work," said President Obama.[1]

Knucklehead is an offensive term that deliberately insults somebody's intelligence or consideration for others. This term minimizes the egregious behavior. This is typical of the normalized cultural response to the pandemic of purchasing sex, even with children.

Everyday there are arrests and scandals for men and women having sex with commercial sex workers and with children being prostituted. The

1 http://abcnews.go.com/blogs/politics/2012/04/knuckleheads-shouldnt-diminish-secret-service-obama-says/

use of commercial sex is pervasive in our military and other trusted institutions. Part of the problem is that many do not yet connect human trafficking, sex trafficking, and prostitution as co-related criminal enterprises.

We must demand better of our government officials and leaders. The same is true in the church. If the church does not take a stand internally, it will have no voice externally. Is your pastor speaking on this subject? Perhaps you need to ask why not. There are very good resources available to assist pastors in constructing appropriate messages as well as conducting Bible studies on these sensitive issues.

Responding Proactively

Prayer is one of the most important parts of our response. Prayer for Freedom[1] is an organization that is actively engaging in the world. In their newsletter Joy Brooks said: *I met one of the leaders of the ministry who shared her heart and the changes that can happen to help prevent slavery. This young woman, in her 20's, gets to the shelter before 7 AM to prepare lunch for 30-70 kids each day. She shares the love of Christ and encourages*

---

1   http://www.prayerforfreedom.com

children and teenagers to trust in God in the most difficult of situations.

As I met with her she told me don't do anything because you believe it is "good, do it because you believe it is God's will." Many times, I have met people who looked to the Western world for money and answers but here was one of the most humble and godly women I have ever met. She knew that only if it was the will of God would it work. Right now, this woman is praying for us and we are praying for her and the ministry she does, to know exactly what the will of God is to bring change to children enslaved and to work together knowing that only through dependence on God will we be able to change lives.

My prayer is that you will find what you own in the issues of trafficking and that you will find what you believe is "God's will." Trafficking is our travesty and must be taken personally and corporately as believers.

Comprehensive Response Strategy

We have looked, so far, at the "why" to respond to trafficking as a calling from God, our ownership or contributions, and our responsibilities. Now we will explore the "what" and "how" to respond more strategically. The four chapters Prevention, Intervention, Education, and Restoration (PIER) each will include both labor and sex trafficking within the topic. You will notice some overlapping pieces.

People often ask me to tell them what they should do next. The fact of the matter is I can describe the four PIER areas but it is going to take a concerted time of prayer and listening to God's direction before they know which avenue to take. Just as Moses went to the elders and all of them proceeded to take three days to pray and fast in the desert to hear God's directions. People who feel compelled to respond must take the time to get still before the Lord and have Him reveal their gifts, talents, and abilities He has designed for their response to "fit." There are a myriad of organizations now that did not even exist five years ago. Please be sure to read the section on the HOPE Matrix to find or start an organization that is compatible with your calling.

Abolitionists also need to have good self-care and a team of folks who will come around them as the eldership did for Moses. While Moses was the leader, he had a group that surrounded him with prayer and fasting. They listened to God together for discernment, wisdom, and direction. No one who confronts evil will be unscathed by the enemy. Each participant must have a network of caring individuals praying for them and practice the disciplines of a Christian life that will help them to be closely aligned with God's heart.

The abolitionists' networks are becoming stronger and more cohesive. They are offering summits and retreats. Some of those include Exodus Cry's Abolitionist Summit in Kansas City[1] and the International Christian Alliance on Prostitu-

---

1 www.exoduscry.com

tion, which meets every four years in Green Lake Wisconsin.[1]

Specialized care and training by professionals is a hallmark of a group that is focusing on the needs of the abolitionist. Counselors and educators that teach the art and science of healthy spirituality and self-care are important to look for in a conference. One of the best in this area is Dr. Dan Allender.[2] Materials are also available from the Faith Alliance Against Slavery and Trafficking for those who provide direct care for victims. "Hands that Heal" is a wonderful curriculum and provides options for taking care of the caregivers.[3]

Lastly, find a mentor! Someone who is perhaps older but definitely more experienced in following the Lord. A person of the same gender is preferable for many reasons. This needs to be someone with wisdom and authenticity. Someone who will laugh with you, cry with you, and help to right your boat when you are tipped over in the storms of life. Find that individual who is in the relationship to point you back to God's Word, to His counsel, to worship Him. This person should be

1 http://www.icapglobal.org/

2 See his website and books for those that care for others. http://theallendercenter.org/wounded-heart/

3 http://www.faastinternational.org/#/hands-that-heal

one who will praise you when you need and not flinch to call you to account. Never give up looking for those that will stand with you when you are reeling from a red-light visit that left you sick to your stomach. Pursue Godly relationships that bring you closer to Him while you march into the depths of the depravity that is human trafficking. Search for these people in your life like precious jewels. You will need them.

You will need to become this kind of mentor for someone else. God will use you to speak into other people's lives and to cheer them toward the prize. Be present and real and you will find those people you can speak blessing and encouragement to along your path.

Prevention

Smokey the Bear was made famous decades ago with this special slogan "Only you can prevent forest fires." Our national forests post his image and that slogan on nearly every entrance. We should apply that slogan to trafficking and our consumer habits. "Only you can prevent human trafficking!" An icon like Smokey would resonate in people's visual memory. It is going to take every one of us making changes and demanding changes. We have to remove the "fuel" that the fire uses.

Prevention is one of the consistently missing essential pieces of the anti-trafficking puzzle. This is especially true for the sex industry, which we will address later in this chapter. First, we will look at prevention in the labor trafficking area.

Caveat Emptor

The question of why we buy what we buy and for what purposes is a discussion of the heart. What is it we are seeking with our consumerism? Does pride and comparison to others drive us to buy more designer named articles? We might be comparing ourselves with others in unhealthy and sinful ways. Our journey must include a self-evaluation of our buying and spending habits as well as our stewardship of the resources God has entrusted to us. Please do not dismiss this aspect. Personally, you must come to grips with your consumer habits. Ask God to show you if you need to change your heart and mind about your buying habits.[1]

Consumers can prevent contributing to labor trafficking. We must know the supply chains of our goods and services. We are the last link on the supply chain as we buy products from the global market. We must investigate if the companies that produce the products are monitored for exploitation and trafficking. You can buy smarter for just

---

[1] Resources to study Biblical stewardship are available through the National Christian Foundation, Financial Peace University, and Crown Financial ministries.

about every product you need and help prevent contributing to exploitation.

I encourage you to explore terms like: farmer exchanges and fair trade or direct trade items as well as slave free. None of those mechanisms of trade is a fail-proof way of knowing that products are without exploitation but knowing the lingo will help. Becoming a wise consumer takes time. Study the options for making better choices in supporting anti-trafficking endeavors and empower entrepreneurial endeavors that assist victims.[1] Dr. Paul Rickert of LeTourneau University cautions that FairTrade is a trademark (hence a business) and not a philosophy as such. The rules inside FairTrade need to be explored for their validity in creating slave free and free trade options. Free trade with access to markets and productivity networks is considered better. Check out Victor Claar's book "Fair Trade? Its Prospects as a Poverty Solution."

Study the concepts of business as mission and empowerment of entrepreneurs in the local community to create a sustainable business that

---

1 See the following organizations websites for more information on their efforts: http://tradeasone.com/, http://goodnewsgoods.com/, http://www.worldcraftsvillage.com/

reduces the risks of individuals and families. So-lutions must be carefully thought through. I encourage you to consider our Western problem-solving perspective: "We need to do something even if it doesn't work or even if it's the wrong thing" because some things we try, may actually be harmful. Good intentions often have unintended consequences, though they satisfy our heart-need to help in some tangible way.

Demand drives the market. Simple economics also apply to the sex industry. If you remove the demand for the product, the supply will also dwindle. Drs. Ed Schauer, Elizabeth Wheaton, and Thomas Galli, have a paper available online called "Economics of Human Trafficking." I encourage you to read it to understand the global economic impacts of trafficking.[1] Learn more about how companies you purchase from are doing in how they check to insure that their supply chain is slave free or fair trade.[2]

---

1   http://onlinelibrary.wiley.com/doi/10.1111/j.1468-2435.2009.00592.x/abstract

2   See these websites for more information: www.betterworldshopper.org and www.free2work.org/. There are apps for your smart phone to use while shopping from Free2work, too.

You can find some products through a global supply chain established to assist formerly exploited workers.[1] They also have collaborated with other nonprofit organizations to develop and market to churches and communities.[2] This is one simple way to encourage your congregation toward prevention of trafficking.

Cheaper labor costs are also part of the problem of exploitation for farm workers, construction workers, domestic workers (maid/nanny) and restaurant workers, and other venues. Research and active engagement can also help you know the extent of this issue. The Immokalee Farm Workers Union in Florida has been addressing the farm workers issues for several years.[3] You can learn how to know which corporations are socially responsible with their supply chains and employees.[4]

Pablo, from a poor Honduran family, heard about job opportunities in Cincinnati, Ohio. He joined others pursuing the American dream, only

---

1   Check this sample organization: www.tradeasone.org.

2   One example is www.goodnewsgoods.com.

3   www.ciw-online.org/

4   Two organizations that can assist you in understanding these issues globally: www.freetheslaves.net and www.notforsalecampaign.org.

to have his journey end abruptly in Austin, Texas. Betrayed by those who promised help and transportation, Pablo became another statistic of the thousands of victims of human trafficking. Pablo's story, however, has a happy ending of being rescued by people unhindered in their efforts to make a difference in their community.

Rescuing men and women, children, teenagers, or entire families seeking asylum or work, takes an unhindered spirit of willingness to stop human trafficking. Whether it is a teenage runaway or one kicked out of the home, even American youth are exploited and enslaved before your eyes.[1]

Consider checking out the businesses in your community for possible use of exploited workers. Asking questions at the nail salon may make a business owner think twice and prevent exploitive practices. There is a list of questions on the Human Trafficking Resource Center website,[2] and you can always call with questions about what you might be observing 1-888-3737-888.

---

1   December 2010, Missions Mosaic, Go & Do Feature, "Human Trafficking in My Community? What Can I Do?" by Virginia Kreimeyer.

2   www.polarisproject.org

A word of caution here: what you are learning does not make you a rescue expert. You must be vigilant without becoming a vigilante. If you suspect anything, make a call to the hotline listed above. If you believe someone in a business is in imminent danger call 911. DO NOT try to rescue someone you think might be a trafficking victim. It is dangerous for you and them.

Preventing trafficking has become a campaign area that various governmental agencies are taking more seriously. They have produced online training for first responders, medical, and law enforcement personnel. They have video trainings targeted to Mexican travelers, which are used for preventing people from being tricked by traffickers or smugglers who promise them a job and great earnings but are not true once they are in the U.S. These materials are accessible from various websites of the federal government.[1]

Education for medical personnel is available. Nurses and doctors can learn about the signs and medical indicators of exploitation. There is an online curriculum available through the Christian Medical Dental Association. CMDA: "Trafficking in

---

1   www.dhs.gov/files/programs/human-trafficking-awareness-training.shtm

Persons: A Primer for the Health Care
Professional."[1]

Prevention of sexual abuse, which creates vulnerabilities for children, is a natural fit for church-
es. They can do
training for their
own children and
open the training

> *The Lord is known by his justice;*
> *the wicked are ensnared by the*
> *work of their hands.*
> *Proverbs 9:16*

up for community members. Guidance is available
for trainers in the "Stewards of Children" curriculum from Darkness to Light.[2]

Prevention of personal exposure to the elements of sexual services as a commodity to be
bought and sold on the open market is a first step.
Here are some of the places you will find the cul-
prits: Internet, magazines, movies, television, videos, children's toys, commercials, books, clothing,
etc. You will find "sex sells" and "anything goes"
marketing in almost every medium. You would
have to live in a bubble without access to the
world in order to insulate yourself. Here is how

1 http://www.cmda.org/WCM/CMDA/Navigation/Hu-
man_Trafficking/TIP_Module_Descriptions.aspx

2 www.d2l.org

you can minimize the exposures for yourself and others in your community:

Prevent personal exposure by

- What you tolerate in your television shows–Really, what are you watching?
- Not supporting businesses that advertise with sexualized messages–we'll talk more about this in the intervention section through emails, letters, petitions.
- What you buy in the following: clothing, magazines, movies, videos, children's toys.
- Do not buy porn or tolerate others talking about porn in conversations as if it is acceptable (we'll talk about educating others on this in a later chapter).
- Think about what is coming to your eyes and ears and reject those that are sexualized–set up personal parameters of acceptability and accountability.
- Prevent children in your care from being exposed to pornography and sexual abuse
- Prevent the silence that is so pervasive concerning issues of sexual abuse.

Intervention

What does intervention look like for the ordinary individual as opposed to the "special ops" trained military expert? Intervention is firmly rooted in vigilance and often looks like active advocacy.

Sexually Oriented Businesses (SOBs), for example, are open in communities that have allowed them to operate. The city or county in which they conduct business can be asked by its citizens to stop allowing SOBs to exist by ordinance or law. The billboards that advertise such establishments could be removed by wise intervention. The community standards for decency dictate what is acceptable. Intervention can be used to raise the standards where you live. There are legal means to get businesses like these closed. Respectful intervention will go a long way. See the list and examples below.

As we focus on the ideals and goals of intervention in human trafficking, let me be perfectly clear about what this does NOT mean. It does not mean suddenly you are the character played by Liam Neeson in the movie "Taken" on a mission to single-handedly rescue victims and eradicate everyone in your way. Citizens should be vigilant not vigilante in their approach.

Traffickers are in this enterprise for the money and power. It is not safe for an untrained person to try to intervene on behalf of a victim. As heroic and glamorous as that might seem, you may end up being killed and/or getting the victim beaten or killed. Traffickers do not care who you are unless you are a paying customer or you interrupt their money stream. They have the mentality, the means, and the capacity to respond with deadly force. You must rely on law enforcement and trained professionals to do rescues.

Here are some suggestions for appropriate intervention:

Through the public arena you can actively ask for:

- Changes to applicable city ordinances

- Changes to or strengthening state laws concerning trafficking–most legislatures are taking this seriously and making great headway[1]
- Changes to businesses that are complicit in using force, fraud, and coercion on workers whether they are domestic, legal, or illegal immigrants
- Corporations to take responsibility and create policies that check supply chains for exploitation of workers[2]
- Corporations that implement training for their workers to spot victims of trafficking in their establishments (hotels, taxis, agricultural work, etc.)
- Corporations that do not allow for the presence of sex trafficking or prostitution and their complicity in such known activities
- Corporations to sign the "No Porn" initiative to not make pornography accessible

---

1   See Shared Hope's "Protected Innocence Report" http://www.sharedhope.org/WhatWeDo/BringJustice/ PolicyRecommendations/ProtectedInnocenceInitiative. aspx

2   www.free2work.org

- Corporations to have "business entertainment" policies that prohibit engagement by their employees and as entertainment for clients
- Travel agencies and entities that do not establish travel for sex tourism or condone it[1]
- Enforcement of existing laws at federal level concerning pornography, especially those of children being raped molested, etc.

Federal funding for victims, reauthorization of the Trafficking Victims' Protection Act and other domestic legislation.[2]

One example of an organization that is doing excellent work with intervention approaches is Free the Captives, started by Julie Waters. Julie has a strategic plan to involve various churches by offering several points of engagement. Free the Captives focuses on (1) AFTERCARE by providing direct services to trafficked teenaged victims, (2) PREVENTION through programming for at-risk teenage girls, (3) DETERRENCE through reducing the demand by focusing on the buyers/Johns

---

1   http://www.thecode.org

2   Check out the video to see how easy this is: http://www.traffickstop.org/page/advocate-policy-makers

through their "Buy Sex? Bye, bye Freedom!" billboard, radio and TV campaign, and (4) AWARENESS by educating thousands of people each year in Houston through their annual conference and trainings.

Through these four goals, Free the Captives is generating ways for the church and the community at large to be hands on involved in the fight against human trafficking that is both safe and effective. For example, Free the Captives has focused a great deal on the demand side of human trafficking. Their work has elevated the scrutiny that law enforcement and prosecutors place on the Johns. For the longest time, in Houston, the focus of anti-trafficking work was on the victims and the traffickers. The Johns, a necessary third party for trafficking to occur, were largely overlooked. In their work with teenage victims, Free the Captives realized that something must be done about the Johns or their work with the victims would be never ending. It was an issue of supply and demand. As long as the Johns demanded young flesh, traffickers would continue to go out and enslave young girls.

Thus, Free the Captives launched a two year long campaign to tackle the issue of the demand. It first started out with a letter writing campaign to Houston's mayor, district attorney, police department and Sheriff's Office. Some officials responded more positively than others. Free the Captives kept the pressure on these elected officials and within a year, over 15,000 letters had been mailed to city and state officials. Harris County Sheriff Adrian Garcia responded positively to this public outcry for help. He began conducting reverse prostitution stings in which the Johns or buyers were arrested. Then he released the names and photos of the men arrested. From college students to an oil and gas executive and everyone in between were arrested in the stings. After these reverse stings, Free the Captives began to ask the public to send "thank you" notes to law enforcement. Sheriff Garcia and his Vice Department have received hundreds of handwritten thank you notes for their proactive work in going after the Johns.

Additionally, Free the Captives also launched a billboard and television campaign that focused specifically on the role that Johns were playing in fueling sex trafficking. Free the Captives' projects are geared toward getting people involved and using their God-given talents to make a difference.

Something as small as writing a letter makes a significant difference!

Lastly, Julie is trained as an attorney and has offered training and organized pro bono work with fellow attorneys in the area. Her work is amazing and an excellent representation of God as they endeavor to intervene in Houston.[1]

Hidden in plain sight, human trafficking is a monstrous crime that law enforcement alone cannot eradicate. No other criminal enterprise has ever before forced open the doors for citizens, churches, civic, and non-profit organizations to form partnerships with local law enforcement agencies to address an issue. Law enforcement has recognized they need the allies in the local community in order to provide them reliable information but more importantly to offer care and restoration for rescued victims.

Community-oriented policing strategies have been common in recent law enforcement efforts to engage the community in solving problems with crime. Human trafficking advocates have turned the tables though. It is new for law enforcement to have the community's organizations ask them

---

1   www.freethecaptiveshouston.com

to gather with them to formulate a pre-planned response.

Coalitions of stakeholders have formed all across the United States with various organizations. Law enforcement can engage with groups to provide appropriate knowledge and to formulate a plan to react when a citizen recognizes a situation. They teach citizens vigilance, but do not create vigilantes. This helps citizens avoid danger and prevents the creation of other unnecessary issues for law enforcement officers.

The church can and should play an integral role in leadership for a local community effort. As a bridge into the community, the church can provide professionals with an open door to their facility and opportunities to educate its members and community leaders. The churches can also work together to gather a network of stakeholders. They can recruit partners from non-governmental organizations (NGO's), medical professionals, service providers, educators, and homeless networks, to work with law enforcement.

The stakeholders can learn together how to educate the community to see and recognize trafficking victims. Additionally, they can form partnerships and alliances to be ready before any victims are located–to have a system in place to provide victim-centered care. In coalitions the stakeholders learn from each other and bring unique assets to the table.

First Baptist Church in Commerce, Texas, has begun a work in their local community to accomplish this. The church offered training for their membership on human trafficking. Next, they collaborated with the local law enforcement agencies to offer the four-hour mandated training required for Texas' law enforcement officers. The church graciously provided a luncheon for the attendees. The church members were offered the opportunity to participate in this training as well. Officers from various agencies were able to dialogue about what they were learning and interact with the church members.

These officers commented on how they felt appreciated and how grateful they were for the church providing the meal. Hosting events opens doors for collaboration. The church provided the training at no charge to the officers or their departments. This was a service not only to the individual officers but to their agencies as well.

The church has begun to assemble their local stakeholders working with the local university and campus organizations. They offered a concert on Texas A&M Commerce's campus to raise awareness. Next, they can work with the university and the trained officers to strategize and provide further education in the community. They can include local prevention and child advocacy groups to teach children and their parents about safety and protection from online predators.

The church campus can be the hub for training events and community forums. Auditoriums of the church could be used for presentations and screening of films such as "Nefarious: Merchants of Souls" by Exodus Cry.[1] Many other documentaries also exist to provide other options.[2]

The possibilities for the church to engage with the law enforcement community are endless. It is fundamentally about building relationships, learning from each other, and building trust. Fulfilling a mission of justice is a bold and courageous endeavor for the local church. This is at the very core of the Church's mission as a part of bringing justice to their community and beyond.

Larry Megason's story from earlier was just the beginning of Restore A Voice in Austin. He

---

1 http://nefariousdocumentary.com/

2 http://aheartforjustice.com/

found God's divine direction, connections, and collaboration that only God could have provided. He tells the story of how God catapulted the work of RAV to a completely new level through their engagement with law enforcement and others.

In January of 2012, I was invited to attend a sub-committee meeting of the Central Texas Coalition Against Human Trafficking. I had been given clear directions to "listen and learn." Normally, I am a good listener and a lifetime learner and this should not have been a problem. However, that did not happen at this meeting.

Before the meeting, I had done my homework. This Coalition is the best and the brightest in their fields of service, including the Office of the State Attorney General, Child Protective Services, Department of Family Protective Services, Refugee Services of Texas, non-governmental organizations, grant writers, sexual assault experts, and more other experts. They are good at what they do. They bring intelligence and passion to the conversation.

I reminded myself that I came to this meeting to "listen and learn." Inexplicably I could not be silent. Questions began gnawing at me. Pieces of the puzzle did not fit together.

We were specifically discussing the need for an aftercare solution for Domestic Minor Sex Trafficking (DMST), minors who were sexually trafficked. Not so timidly, I raised my hand, introduced myself, and asked this question, "During all of the years of funding, why hasn't this organization provided the solution?"

The silence was deafening. After what seemed several minutes, the leader of the meeting looked at me and another man and simply said, "You're now in charge of getting us a home!"

In my naiveté I thought, "How hard can this be? Get a house, put up a sign, and invite the girls to come in."

In the days that followed, my team very gently began to guide me through the bureaucratic, social service, victim service, law enforcement, and the endless maze of red tape! It was then that my strategic wiring really kicked in and Restore A Voice began the slow burn of due diligence, undergirded by prayer, that brought us to God's plan.

A few months later, I found myself sitting at a table in the Cedar Park Police headquarters surrounded by forty-plus law enforcement personnel from around central Texas and beyond. The who's who of law enforcement was there: Texas Rangers, the Department of Public Safety, Federal agencies (FBI, Homeland Security), and Austin police department. Austin has an exceptional Human Trafficking Unit and had invited many other local police departments to be present as well.

We gathered to prepare for the largest international sporting event in America. Formula One racing would be in Austin within a few months. As the "strike force" began to lay out their plans citing the significant collaborative effort of so many in law enforcement, one lead detective asked the question no one could answer; "When we rescue a minor during this event, what are we going to do with her?"

As I looked around the room at the very best law enforcement, victim services, CPS and more, I lifted my hand and said, "I'm not quite sure what we're going to do, but I'll take them."

I am sure my team thought, "There he goes again! What are we going to do with him?"

What happened in the next few months cannot be explained in any way other than God had His fingerprints all over the process. At that meeting, law enforcement estimated between 15 and 50 minor girls would be rescued. The solution had to be delivered with guarantees. Restore A Voice quickly *learned that it was also going to be expensive. The details of the next few weeks seem like a blur as I look back, but it was amazing what God did.*

A full month before the race, our efforts had been completely funded, we had a safe house for any and all that were rescued, and we had secured referral homes in other parts of the country where the girls could receive long-term care to guide them back to a full, free life.

Additionally, the Restore A Voice team and volunteers spent the final few weeks preparing to serve the various law enforcement agencies at the command post providing around-the-clock coffee, fruit, pastries, water, sodas and more. We came to serve the servants.

Other volunteers from churches and campus organizations purchased and prepared care packages for 50 girls. Each care package had hygiene products, shampoo, lotion, underwear, sweat pants, a blanket, a stuffed animal, and more. The preparation room was filled with people from around the region. Many different churches, the youth, children, moms, and dads served together. It was incredible.

Prayer played a key role in all that was accomplished. A teen girls group and their advisors helped to facilitate an educational piece and asked the churches to pray before and during the events.

The University of Texas School of Social Work, in partnership with the local Coalition said unequivocally that this was the finest expression of collaboration the city had ever seen concerning this issue. Restore A Voice realized these were God's divine appointments and activities.

Restore A Voice has been birthed over literally a thousand cups of coffee where we have shared the story and vision repeatedly. It has been slow, intentional building of strategic alliances and partnerships with like-minded people and groups. It has been the meticulous hours of asking the hard questions and getting harder answers. It has been prayer meetings and personal prayer times bombarding the heavens petitioning God for wisdom, compassion, and brokenness for those we serve. It has been costly on many levels of sacrifice. We have gladly stood on our relationship with Jesus Christ knowing He would always guide, always provide, always sustain, and always remain with us. We do this because we cannot do anything else. We do it for the glory of our heavenly Father. At the end of every day, remember, "IT'S FOR THE GIRLS!"

Expanding your influence and intervention can also happen personally through your circles of influence with peers, friends, and family members.

- Make wise choices about what you watch (movies, TV, etc.). This may be costly in relationships with others who do not understand why you might be so sensitized to this issue and why you would take such a stand against being victimized or by watching others being exploited.[1]

- Taking a stand about what you eat, what you wear, what you buy, and why you make those choices is a way to advocate that others make smart choices and minimize their footprint in trafficking.[2]

- Provide positive peer pressure that can foster good outcomes. Be intentionally positive and encourage others to make their voices heard about the issues as well.

- Learn to advocate for the collective good of the abolition movement and help others who have campaigns. Find out where your

---

1 www.socialcostsofpornography.org

2 See more at www.slaveryfootprint.org and www.free-2work.org

gifts, skills, talents, and passions may be useful in the movement.[1]

- Learn about and promote the strong work being done around the world in advocating for victims and for caring for their needs. We will address restoration specifically in a later chapter.

For those of you who are called to the political arena there are options to intervene. Legislative intervention is the mechanism for being engaged on local, state, and federal levels. Find out through your local children's advocacy groups, prevention groups, and elected officials what ordinances, bills, or legislation are being discussed. Take groups to the meetings and advocate for new laws and system changes to correct problems and then make your voice heard on behalf of the voiceless. The Christian Life Commission in Texas carefully monitors legislative efforts in Austin and can give guidance on engagement. Check with your denominational leaders to see if there is a group working in your state.

International Justice Mission is one of the best experts in legal intervention. They have a robust

---

1   http://www.notforsalecampaign.org/empower/

means of preparation and support for their personnel. Law students and attorneys can find many opportunities with IJM.[1]

In the US context, law enforcement has had a difficult time working with zealous organizations and individuals. The vigilante "Rambo" character has been squashed as well as operations that want to infiltrate criminal enterprises or attempt rescue of victims. Several of these organizations have had to re-think their strategy for lack of acceptance and for high liability reasons.

If you have credentials from the military or specialized law enforcement training, I would suggest you consider the programs available for such specialties through the National Center for Missing and Exploited Children.[2] Please do not become a vigilante. It may cost your life or the life of a trafficking victim. Remember, Moses did not go alone to Pharaoh; he and his brother had a God given plan.

An educational initiative known as Traffick-Stop functions as a MANGO. No, this is not referring to the wonderful tropical fruit, but mobilization/advocacy NGO's. Increasing societal

---

1   www.ijm.org

2   www.ncmec.org

awareness of human trafficking over the last few years is both due to and resulting in the growth of a different type of NGO: those focused on mobilizing citizens against human trafficking and on (mostly) local and state-level advocacy for stronger anti-trafficking laws and better services for trafficking victims. These mobilization/advocacy NGO's (MANGOs) rarely, if ever, provide direct services for victims and, thus, may not have any direct contact with law enforcement or other government entities.[1]

In my work, I serve as an educator and connector for community organizations that focus on human trafficking in the U.S. context. Training for the majority of my work are focused on Domestic Minor Sex Trafficking also known as Commercial Sexual Exploitation of Children. The work brokers information across various disciplines focusing on prevention of sexual abuse, intervention techniques, education and awareness of the related issues, and the need for restorative care for victims. This work fills a unique niche of bridging for NGO's, medical professionals, service providers,

1 Law Enforcement Executive Forum, Vol. 12, No.1, March 2012 by John Vanek and Kirsten Foot. (http://traccc.gmu.edu/pdfs/Law_Enforcement_Executive_Forum.pdf#page=8)

educators, homeless networks, and others to law enforcement as well as governmental agencies.

These are just a few suggestions for vigilant intervention. There are countless ways for individuals to take their passions and respond to the issues of human trafficking. Bring these issues to your peer group, family members, church, or community as a natural extension of your personal choices, your profession, and your passion. Your one voice can make a difference as you consider your role, responsibility, and response to trafficking.

> *How, then, can they call on the one they have not believed in? And how can they believe in the one of whom they have not heard? And how can they hear without someone preaching to them? And how can they preach unless they are sent? As it is written, "How beautiful are the feet of those who bring good news!"*
> *Romans 10:14-15*

Education

Education is key to people being aware of the problems of human trafficking and it ties to the mission Christ proclaimed. Remember, the good news is what Jesus said in Luke 4:18 *"...to proclaim freedom . . . to release the oppressed."* The educational aspect of Jesus' ministry and the mission itself are two-sides of the same coin. They represent the why and the how of a Christian's purposed life.

Generally in Christendom, we have taken on the Great Commission challenge to preach the good news from Matthew 28:19, *"Therefore, go and make disciples of all nations, baptizing them in the name of the Father and of the Son and of the Holy Spirit, and teaching them to obey everything I have commanded you. And surely I am with you always, to the very end of the age."* This is coupled with Acts 1:8, which tells us where to go to make disciples: *"But you will receive power when the Holy Spirit comes on you; and you will be my witnesses in Jerusalem, and in all Judea and Samaria, and to the ends of the earth."*

Somewhere over the centuries we have reduced the good news mission to preaching salvation, sealing the deal of a decision for Christ, (notches on a belt) throwing money at the problems, and sending missionary endeavors (both long and short-term). Rarely has education involved discipleship that is life altering, problem solving, and community changing. There are some exceptional endeavors but for the most part few missional engagements have produced such results.

I believe it is because we are derailed from the mission Christ proclaimed and do not stay focused on the ultimate goal but rather the number of salvations recorded. For years in addressing community missions and benevolence work, I heard the old adage: "Give a man a fish, feed him for a day. Teach a man to fish, feed him for a lifetime."

I have learned there are several more parts to complete the full message: "Introduce the man to the Creator of the fish, and feed them for all eternity." This however, does not complete the educational work of true discipleship.

There are two more pieces to consider: "Teach the man to be a fisher of men and fulfill the Great Commission."

One last part is needed to produce true transformation that embodies the good news of freedom of which Christ spoke: "Teach the man to own the pond and bring Shalom to his whole community." Ownership includes helping people gain "... access to markets and networks of productivity."[1]

Another whole book would be necessary to unpack those concepts. Nevertheless, we can see more fully the need to know the "why" we respond to human trafficking before we shallowly respond. We must be strategic thinkers about our responsibilities and the church's role in "how" to respond that allows true transformation to take place.

Education as a Response

Human trafficking is complex and involves a multitude of contributing factors. In the global context, poverty plays a large role. In impoverished communities that have few

---

1   Michael Matheson Miller, www.povertycure.org

resources for their members it is not easy to resist bogus "opportunities" that lure them and their children into trafficking situations.

Many governments are even complicit in the disguise of trafficking in and through their countries because of a floundering economy and gross national product that relies on the commoditization of their citizenry. Lack of developmental resources and natural resources also play a role. Conflict and war serve to increase and bring increased poverty and in turn vulnerability of women and children.

In the despair of poverty often resides a spark of hope for a better life—if not a better life for the parent, then one for their children. This is the very fuel that a trafficking recruiter will use: a promise made to fulfill that sense of hope for a better life, for food to eat, for the prospects of a lucrative job, and money to be sent home to help the family. Parents, families, and communities must be taught about these deceptions.

Curriculum must include the realities of deceitful practices used on children. The family must learn that the sense of hope and the promise of so much is the very dream that turns to disaster and desperation on the other side of the false promise.

Children often have no choice. They believe their parents are doing a good thing. They aspire to hope. They want be a good child for their parents. False hope is soon revealed when the child experiences inhumane treatment at the hands of adults and even other children. Children are also assigned as recruiters or manipulators to deceive, abuse, and extinguish hope for new victims. Education should teach prevention and restoration are possible.

Trafficking Intersects a Family

Sandy Shepherd is a pre-school teacher from Colleyville, Texas, an affluent community outside of Fort Worth. How could a wife and mother of three daughters become involved in the redemptive process of human trafficking? Before she knew what human trafficking was, Shepherd answered God's call to, *"love your neighbor as yourself."* (Matt. 22:39) Even though the neighbor she learned to love was from a country a world away, "my faith was my guiding rod," she said.

Shepherd's church, First Baptist of Colleyville, had arranged for the Zambia Acappella Boys Choir (ZABC) to perform as part of their tour in the U.S. in 1996. Over the course of several years of hosting the choir members in their home, Sandy said she and her husband Deetz, "fell in love with the kids, loved their music, and heard their stories." It was during the process of asking normal questions about the boys as they told their stories, when Shepherd and other host families began to sense something terribly wrong.

Keith Grimes, a Baptist missionary to Zambia, promised the choristers' families to bring the boys to America to earn money and an education, something that was next to impossible in Zambia. What the Shepherds and other host families learned was that Grimes did not fulfill his promises but exploited and controlled the boys' time, money and access to their families. "He had a violent temper," Shepherd explained. "The more host families became involved, the more controlling he became. He frequently threatened to deport the boys. The crowning blow came when we were going to have them at Christmas in 1997." Grimes' plan, which he confided in Shepherd, was to send seven of the singers home in disgrace without warning and without anything but a duffle bag.

"I told him he had to prepare them psychologically and to change their diet from hamburgers and french fries to prepare them for eating nshima, a corn meal dish, they would get only once a day. However, Grimes did not listen and in January 1998 seven boys went home to be outcast by their families. They went from living in American homes to having no place at all. While they loved nshima, the sudden change in diet created weeks of stomach problems and their weight dropped quickly," she said.

In June, when all 26 had been returned to Zambia, Shepherd refused to have anything else to do with Grimes or the ZABC. Instead, she wrote letters to the U.S. Attorney General, was interviewed by the FBI, and lodged complaints against Grimes' ministry for his treatment of the choristers.

But her heart went out to those who returned to Zambia where they would not be educated. She began a fundraising campaign for a high school for about 26 boys. That was where she began to focus her energy and time, even making trips to Zambia to ensure the arrangements were meeting the boys' needs.

However, in the spring of 1999, Grimes died and his daughter and her husband assumed control of ZABC. A year later Grimes' daughter, Barbara Grimes Martens, threatened to call the Immigration and Naturalization Service (INS) in order to deport seven more boys for not following the rules in the choir's handbook after a performance in Texas. Circumstances had deteriorated and the boys told the INS agents they would rather be in jail than return to the ZABC. A very compassionate INS officer did not want to see the boys stay in jail, so he called the Colleyville Baptist Church. When a Deacon at Shepherd's church called her, she was on her way to her daughter's high school.

"I did not understand why the Lord was calling me back to working with the choir and least of all someone who had called me a witch," she said. Her focus was now on the Zambian school. "I walked around my house asking, 'God, why are you calling me back to be involved with the boys' choir again?'"

When Shepherd walked into the church and saw the seven boys standing in a circle with two INS officers, an ugly scene ensued with Grimes' son-in-law. The result was that she took all seven home with her for the night. The following Sunday, Shepherd told her Sunday school class that she needed help to find homes for the boys.

It took three months to find homes for all seven boys. Four months later, Given Kachepa, one of the boys, revisited her home and while there, received a letter from his host mom indicating that she could no longer keep him. With a couple of pairs of shorts and shirts, it was time for school to start and Sandy said to Given, "I don't know a family or place for you to go, so we'll start school and see what God has in store."

And that's how Given found his way from being a victim of human trafficking to becoming a survivor through Shepherd's willingness to say, "Yes, Lord, Yes."

Those were the words to a song Shepherd had sung with her choir at FBC Colleyville, but they became her mantra when God called her to love and "changed my life by broadening my perspective," she said. "I don't consider myself any different than anyone else."

From a personal perspective of one who did not even know what human trafficking was, Shepherd advises others to, "Look beneath the surface and ask questions so the person knows you care. Be compassionate," she stresses, "enough to reach out and let others know you care. Have a general awareness [of their situation] and have a Christian attitude."

"I never thought I'd have a son, and now I found myself with a color and culturally different young man who grew in my heart and became my son," she said. "But God has been glorified through Given," she notes. Given's natural mother died when he was seven and his father died when he was nine, but he still has three older brothers and two sisters. He stays in contact with his siblings in Zambia, but shares his life in America with the Shepherds, who love him like the son and brother he is to them.

Given graduated from the University of North Texas with a degree in biology and is attending dental school so he can, "give others a happy smile," like he had when his braces came off. Given has truly become a part of the Shepherd family, though they never adopted him. He has received a green card (or permanent residence) and has finally been able travel to see his family and return to the U.S. to complete his studies.

Trafficking became a real part of the Shepherd family through Given. They have been a part of the Rescue and Restore national human trafficking education campaign.[1] Sandy Shepherd continues to educate others on the issues of human trafficking and to tell their story. She warns, "If you think

---

1   You can see the campaign video at http://www.youtube.com/watch?v=bqyzW84I3Dc (Given's story starts at 6:42

someone is a victim of human trafficking, call the Trafficking Information and Referral Hotline at 1-888-3737-888. You can make a difference."

Special Considerations

Abuse and historical practices of caste systems continues to play a role in some countries. Historical familial debt bondage is also a problem. Also, trickery by traffickers who may offer services that seem legitimate and once the service, such as transportation, is provided then additional fees are levied and a cycle of debt without remedy begins. Distinct class and social hierarchy may be legitimized in some countries, contexts, and cultures that perpetuate servitude and slavery.

Risk factors in some countries are war, medical pandemics such as HIV/AIDS, and other economic crises. The mitigation of circumstances in these countries is often dependent on corrupt governments who do not pass along aid from other countries and interrupt aid from NGO's. The NGO's that are global partners often must look for means and mechanisms for getting resources through government inspectors and rigorous scrutiny.

Solutions for sustainability must include mechanisms of mobilization of goods, products,

and services that are legitimate and create opportunities that are resistant to hostilities within
the countries. Such solutions include education of
the people in their local communities that build
empowerment not just relief. Great resources on
creation of these types of endeavors are available through NGO's such as World Vision,[1] which
is listed as a partner with the United Nations resources for intervention. Training for Global and
US constituents on development models is also
available through the Chalmers Institute[2] and especially their curriculum, "When Helping Hurts."[3]

Interdependence and the marketing of goods
and services in a way that allows for a livable wage
and proper treatment of people are a hallmark of
mechanisms that interrupt trafficking. The market and demand for goods and services should be
responsible to the producers and the consumers
through a cooperative agreement with suppliers
and consumers.

Fair Trade and the development of specialized
markets such as Trade As One[4] serve as models

1   www.worldvision.org
2   www.chalmers.org
3   www.whenhelpinghurts.org
4   www.tradeasone.com

for systemic means to bring together goods and services for those vulnerable to trafficking. However, goods and services that are indigenously supported are much more prudent.[1] An outside solution of giving benevolent "aid" is not always the best solution for the local economy or the businessperson. It can actually do more harm than good. Doing the same old aid and the same old practices of relief are not going to interrupt human trafficking adequately to stop it. We must think differently, act differently, buy differently, support differently![2]

Also, to better understand the value of education as it relates to eradicating women and girls being trafficked be sure to watch the Sheryl Wu-Dunn TED talk listed in the bibliography. She explains how basic education plays a key role in reducing vulnerabilities and creating transformation.[3]

---

1   For more information on the best options of intervention in business solutions based on the needs of the community and what it can support despite global economic impact see: "A Day Without Dignity" http://www.youtube.com/watch?v=isxxQm2_ud0

2   For more information on alternative thinking from the Acton Institute, see www.povertycure.org.

3   http://www.ted.com/talks/lang/eng/sheryl_wudunn_our_century_s_greatest_injustice.html

Educate Yourself and Prepare to Teach

Education is a dynamic and not a static endeavor. The more you learn the more you can teach. After you begin to gain confidence in your knowledge, the next question is "Who do you educate?" I have told people for years that I would tell anyone, anywhere, anytime if they would stand still long enough for me to tell them about human trafficking. I had a colleague, Felipe Garza from Buckner Children and Family Services who challenged me on that. He said, "Do they really have to stand still for you?" We laughed. He was right; it did not even matter to me if someone stopped, I would walk right alongside him or her and tell about trafficking. The watchman on the wall compels me to educate others on this issue. That call is fulfilled wherever God sends me and to whomever He puts in my path.

"Friends, Family, Countrymen lend me your ear" that is a good start. We could also use, Matthew 11:15 *"He who has ears, let him hear."* All kidding aside, the world is your audience but we can break that down into bite-sized pieces.

Educate Your Community

Educating the community about the issues should be strategic and involve as many of the PIER elements (Prevention, Intervention, Education, and Restoration) as possible. An assessment of agencies in your community that work in each of these arenas would help you to know where the gaps are or where you could volunteer to augment their efforts.

Prevention and education go hand-in-hand in local community efforts. Most counties in the US have a children's advocacy center or one nearby that they utilize for community education, prevention seminars, and assisting law enforcement with children who are victims of crime, and more. They would be one of the first agencies you want to look for in knowing what your community has available. Ask if they are looking for volunteers to do community education/awareness training. See if the center offers opportunities for you to be trained. If not, materials are already available that can be used to develop a training program on prevention and awareness education. Websites are all in the Appendix.

Perhaps you are like Moses who told God he was not a good speaker. Reportedly, he stuttered and gave that as an excuse not to respond to God's call. God will not let that be an obstacle. If you want to educate you can do several things to remove this barrier. You can start with reading books, taking mini-courses on public speaking. Perhaps you can find a Toastmaster speakers group through your local Chamber of Commerce or community agency. Ask your friends to help you practice and refine your presentation. Training programs like "Stewards of Children" actually have a "how-to" training session and are video driven so you are mainly facilitating the materials.

Find other organizations and clubs you can speak to and build your presentation and confidence. Put together materials that fit the audience. If it is a local group, you can focus on the issues in the community or the state in which you live. It is as easy as a Google search to find articles on human trafficking by state or city name. You can also ask local advocacy centers or your law enforcement for data on cases—not case details—but the number of cases.

Use everything you learn about your personal footprint to teach. Tell how you came to know about human trafficking and why it has affected you so much. Remember you have this book and many links within it to refer to for information.

Take time to translate how your community can respond. Each community has its mark of slavery and may just be unaware. The CNN Freedom Project has 10 viable steps with education being a key. Get a group of people around you to join in the journey. Here is a portion of the 10 items:[1]

1. Learn about the many signs
2. Assemble a Community Vigilance Committee (CVC)
3. Recruit other community members to join your CVC
4. Make contact with local law enforcement and follow their guidance
5. Make contact with local non-governmental organizations (NGO's)
6. If there are no relevant NGO's or shelters in your area, think about setting one up! (See the later chapter on a matrix to assess organizations)

---

1   http://thecnnfreedomproject.blogs.cnn.com/2011/06/21/community-vigilance-10-steps-people-can-take-to-help-combat-human-trafficking/

7. Create a website in which you share your progress and learning

8. Set up a "Google Alert" for human trafficking

9. Make contact with your local and state lawmakers

10. Report to local law enforcement suspicious activities you recognize

Multiply the effectiveness and support each other by administrating a plan together to make the most of every opportunity. Help educate local companies that employ people from outside the US. They should be meeting the standards for such workers under the federal government rules. The Department of Labor[1] has specific and strict guidelines. If you suspect a company in your community is not following those guidelines or that it is exploiting its workers, report it.

Educate the local hotel/motel businesses about what human trafficking might look like. This is another great way to help the community address its issues. Groups have formed teams to go to local hotels and show them printouts of the children from the National Center for Missing and

---

1   www.dol.gov/

Exploited Children.[1] You can offer to teach them the signs of a child that may be under the control of a pimp and how to report suspicious activity.

One example of this is a group that became known as the "Nun-derground Railroad." This was an order of nuns that went to Indianapolis to educate hotels in preparation for the Superbowl in 2012. This group took on a community education project with over 220 local hotels.[2] The group went one step further and asked the local hotels to pledge to do their part using ECPAT's Code: Code Of Conduct For The Protection Of Children From Sexual Exploitation In Travel And Tourism.[3] There are international hotel chains that have pledged to do their part to minimize child exploitation in their facilities.

These education endeavors on trafficking are repeated in towns and cities all across the United States. The stories you tell in your training can be local, state, national, or international. Do a simple search for news stories on human trafficking and

---

1   www.ncmec.org

2   Read their story published in the Huffington Post: http://www.huffingtonpost.com/2012/01/18/nuns-concerned-about-human-trafficking-super-bowl_n_1213921.html

3   www.thecode.org/

you will find them in every state in the US. National reports on domestic minor sex trafficking can be found at Shared Hope.[1]

In the Schools

Our children typically see their teachers more than they see anyone else outside the home. Teachers hear, see, and observe a great deal of behaviors that they may not recognize as signs of abuse or exploitation. Teachers are a natural audience in your local community. The Polaris Project and youth organizations have resource material available to help them understand the "red flags" of a child that may be victimized. Additional information on specific signs of youth involved in commercial sexual exploitation is available to download or request printed copies.[2]

I have been teaching a four-hour block to educators and have specialized information on vulnerabilities, clues, and cues. Homeless children and youth in our schools are exceptionally susceptible to exploitation. There are many resources available on this issue. Here are a few facts that teachers need to learn.

---

1   www.sharedhope.org
2   http://ncfy.acf.hhs.gov/book/export/html/131

Children who have been sexually abused may display a range of emotional and behavioral reactions characteristic of children who have experienced trauma. These reactions include:

- Increased occurrence of nightmares or other sleeping difficulties
- Withdrawn behavior
- Angry outbursts
- Anxiety
- Depression
- New words for private body parts or sexualized language inappropriate for their age
- Sexual activity with toys or other children
- Not wanting to be left alone with a particular individual(s)

Many sexually abused children exhibit behavioral and emotional changes while others do not. It is critical to focus on recognition of symptom, but it is equally important to address prevention and empowering communication for children. Discussions should include body safety, healthy body boundaries, and empowering the use of open communication about sexual matters.

Children often will not tell about sexual abuse. Here are a few reasons children do not disclose sexual abuse:[1]

- Threats of bodily harm (to the child and/or the child's family–especially siblings)
- Fear of being removed from the home (even if the abuser is a family member) or of their telling being the cause of the family breaking up
- Fear of not being believed
- Shame, guilt, or even being blamed for the incidents

Educate Your Family and Church

Vulnerabilities exist in nearly every family and in all churches. Education must start at home, including your church home. The statistics according to Darkness to Light:

- As many as 60% are abused by people the family trusts—abusers frequently try to form a trusting relationship with parents,

---

1   Adapted from: http://www.nctsn.org/trauma-types/sexual-abuse

including fellow church members or Pastors.

- Nearly 40% are abused by older or larger children
- 30-40% of children are abused by family members

Materials are available to teach children in age appropriate ways about protecting themselves. You cannot be with your children 24 hours a day. The prevention section of this book has recommendations on kid friendly materials to assist you. PureHope.net also has materials to teach from a Biblical perspective.

Your church staff should have policies and procedures to protect the children in their care. If your church does not, you must address it with the pastor and leadership. Most church insurance companies require policies and procedures on dealing with abuse issues. There are very helpful materials available from church insurance companies for training. Policies should require background checks of all workers and volunteers in children and youth areas. A thorough background check should be required for all staff members before hiring. Regular monitoring of the church's security and protection policies can be an opportunity to assist staff in recognizing potential issues.

Education in your church may take a variety of approaches. You could teach about trafficking in Bible Study or home groups and in special settings created to bring awareness to the congregation. Show a documentary video with a discussion time, or invite a panel of experts to follow it with information. Bring a guest speaker to talk about trafficking or someone who represents a reputable anti-trafficking organization in your community or state.

Prayerucation? (Prayer as Education)

Prayer events are a means of education. Prayer is the hardest work in many ways and easiest, most cost effective means of educating others. Small groups can get materials together and share time of prayer or pray individually. A long time ago I learned that prayer is the work and ministry is the reward. If we are not praying, our endeavors will be fruitless. If we expect God to move, we must be praying.

One of the initiatives that God had me start on 10-10-11 at 10 am is called "10 at 10 for I-10."

This is a time set aside on the 10th of every month to pray for the Interstate 10 corridor from Jacksonville, Florida, to Los Angeles, California.[1] The FBI named Interstate 10 the number one trafficking route in the US several years ago. In response to this dubious honor combined with the fact that the largest portion of the highway runs through Texas, the prayer initiative began.

Robin Moore, from Tallowood Baptist Church in Houston, took on the challenge in her local church to rally a group of prayer warriors on the 10th of every month to meet at a location near the Interstate to pray. They know their community and the issues along the stretch nearest to their church. The group has been praying and educating others in their church and community about their efforts. They are praying for victims, traffickers, businesses, consumers, law enforcement, prosecutors, and anyone else involved or effected by this trafficking on Interstate 10.[2]

---

1   Find prayers and information on www.facebook.com/10at10forI10 or on the www.TraffickStop.org website.

2   See this news story on their efforts. http://www.baptiststandard.com/index.php?option=com_content&task=view&id=14318&Itemid=53

From Orange to El Paso, Texas (over 860 miles) the Texas Baptist Convention has over 1,100 affiliated churches within 10 miles of the Interstate-10 corridor. This number does not include any other Christian churches along that route. It is a dream of mine that every mile of Interstate 10 would have a church praying for reducing the demand and eliminating the trafficking of humans and drugs (which are often co-mingled) through Texas.

Elsewhere, I mentioned the prayer event held at Gateway Church in Southlake. They had several hundred women for this event and full program including worship and prayer led by several different organizations. In the great hall outside the worship center, they had booths set up with trusted organizations that gave information, provided for conversations, items for sale, and opportunities to get involved. The organizations represented both local and global partners to find ways to engage. Prayer for Freedom was one of those organizations. They will gladly assist any church or individual who wants to begin to understand or get involved with specific prayer opportunities.[1]

---

1   www.prayerforfreedom.com

A Word to the Men

Prayer as a priority is not just for women. Men must play a significant role in leadership throughout churches to address the issues of demand and to protect the women and children under their watch care. Pastors can help lead the church by setting aside a time to have a concert of prayer specifically about trafficking. Men must be challenged to have their hearts open to God's heart for this issue. The verse that comes to mind is Malachi 4:5: *"See, I will send you the prophet . . . He will turn the hearts of the fathers to their children, and the hearts of the children to their fathers; or else I will come and strike the land with a curse."*

I wonder sometimes where we are with this issue in the world. My prayer is that fathers rise up, now. Fatherlessness and a lack of godly father figures are a complicating factor to the vulnerabilities of all children. Additionally, one in six boys is sexually abused before they turn 18-years-old. Men are hurting and need a place to hope and heal with other men. Groups are desperately needed for men who are dealing with addiction to pornography.[1] Men teaching young men and boys

---

1 I recommend these resources for men on pornography addiction, a video series www.somebodysdaughter.com,

about the dangers of pornography and sexual addiction would be a natural fit for a men's ministry.[1] If you need help, please know that resources exist through online services. I strongly suggest getting your entire family to see a Christian counselor who can assist you on this journey.

A Word for Women

The fastest growing segment of pornography consumers is women and girls. There are also wonderful resources to address this for women's groups and individuals. Look for "Every Woman's Battle" by Shannon Ethridge and the young woman's version by her as well. There are several applicable websites (see links below).[2]There are also helps for families struggling with an addicted family member. Help is available as well through

---

about men and the effect of porn on their lives, families, and ministries. The second is "Porn-Again Christian" by Mark Driscoll (available online as a .pdf file).

1   Other resources exist to teach on sexuality as well include those from www.PureHope.net and "Every Man's Battle" and "Every Young Man's Battle" by Steven Arterburn.

2   www.moralityinmedia.org/ and www.ChristianWomenandPorn.com/, http://pornharms.com/mim/handouts/; http://www.purehope.net/helpline.asp; www.enough.org; http://lighthousenetwork.org/; www.just1clickaway.org; www.somebodysdaughter.org

Enough is Enough, Purehope's helpline, and Josh McDowell's ministry on pornography. If you need help, please know that resources exist through Light House Network and Just 1 Click Away as well as Somebody's Daughter. I would strongly suggest getting your entire family into see a Christian counselor who can assist you on this journey.

Warning Vigilantes will Arise

I have been teaching on this for nearly six years and have realized that this is exasperating information for some audience members. Some have children who may have been victimized; others have been victims as children. Naturally, they have a very emotive response. There have been fathers who have been ready to go to the streets and take matters into their own hands.

The Moses story once again becomes a teaching opportunity in follow-up conversations with highly motivated vigilante-minded activists. Exodus 2:11-14 tells of Moses seeing one of his own people, a Hebrew slave, being beaten by an Egyptian slave master. Moses took matters into his own hands, killed the slave master, and hid his body. He thought no one had seen him. The next day he discovered that he had been seen. When Pharaoh heard what Moses had done he tried to kill Moses, but Moses fled to the desert. He ended up spending 40 years there. I encourage people who are in this mindset to think carefully about the good or harm that their visceral response would bring to them.

I encourage them to take some deep breaths and to learn how to channel that energy more effectively into efforts that would have a long-term effect. They will be more successful and strategic in their endeavors if they will follow Matthew 10:16b *"...be as shrewd as snakes and as innocent as doves."* I sternly warn vigilantes that traffickers are in this criminal enterprise because it is very lucrative. The criminal also has the motivation, means, mentality, and methods to hurt you or kill you and they often do the same to their victim if you try to remove the victim.

Educational efforts can support intervention without crossing the line from vigilant citizen to vigilante. Law enforcement is becoming more aware of the trafficking issue. They are the ones trained to intervene. Citizens can assist law enforcement by gathering very good information about what they see. This includes descriptions of cars or other vehicles, descriptions of the people involved, location information, and anything that is distinctive or indicates a potential trafficking situation. Teach your audience, "If you believe someone is in immediate danger call 911."

Law Enforcement training has not reached every officer. If your local law enforcement agencies have not received training on this issue there are ready to use materials available from several organizations and federal government agencies. Those can be accessed online through the Department of Justice website and the Office of Victims of Crime. I have been training with law enforcement on this issue and most agencies are eager for citizens to provide additional assistance. Many states have developed their own training. Your state's attorney and state police or public safety office may be of assistance in providing training locally as well.

Additionally, teach participants if they have suspicions about something that looks like a potential trafficking situation for example to call the national hotline 888-373-7888. Just one person who knows the signs of someone being trafficked can help initiate a phone call to the national hotline to report something suspicious.

Stories are in the news everyday about ordinary people making a difference. A link is listed below for an example of one vigilant citizen in Largo, Florida, who made a difference. A neighbor saw something was not right when two white vans regularly picked up groups from an apartment. People who have learned about this issue are able to make a simple phone call that can rescue many victims.[1]

One person can make a difference. Will the difference be in your own home or family? Is that you educating your community? Is that you educating your church? Is it you forming a group to pray about this issue? What is the thing you cannot NOT do that tugs on your heart? Find it and do it.

---

1 http://www.tampabay.com/news/publicsafety/ crime/27-people-found-in-human-trafficking-raids-in-largo-clearwater/1138829_

Restoration of Victims
of Trafficking

Restoration services for victims of human trafficking are the most difficult of all the aspects of human trafficking work. It is an intense, long-term, complicated, and costly endeavor. The victims often have medical, psychological, educational, social, and spiritual needs that can require extensive therapy. The continuum of care is still being researched and developed.

"Residential facilities need to be situated along a continuum of care that begins with prevention education and outreach to at-risk populations, teachers and school counselors, health and human services professionals, juvenile justice and child welfare systems personnel, parents and communities at large."[1]

International victims in the US have options for care through the provisions of the Trafficking Victim's Protection Act. Funding has been through several iterations. Locations have been funded for several years across the country. The current funding and systemic fundamental changes have created a situation where fewer service providers are continuing to operate as they have in the past. More information on after-care for victims can be found at The Polaris Project website, which keeps up with where service providers exist and how to contact them.[2] The majority of organizations on this list provide services for internationals.

There are some outstanding and highly reputable organizations that have done victim care for internationals since 2000. These organizations are a part of the list that the Polaris Project manages and you can find that list by your state. One way to figure out if any of these organizations might be right for you to engage with is using the HOPE matrix in a later chapter. Not all organiza-

1 Source: Report to the Department of Health and Human Services, 2007 (17)

2 http://www.polarisproject.org/resources/tools-for-service-providers-and-law-enforcement.

tions work well with integrating volunteers who are offering services.

The local human trafficking taskforces or coalitions need service providers that can walk with victims through their recovery in many ways. Those opportunities may include language service. Providing English as a Second Language classes is often a great opportunity to assist victims. You can connect with local victim assistance groups or through law enforcement's victims programs. This could be an avenue to provide tangible services without having to begin a shelter.

Special Consideration for US Victims

Very few options exist in the United States for children that have been trafficked into commercial sexual exploitation of children (CSEC). It is estimated less than 300 beds are currently available in residential aftercare for victims. The estimated cost of housing a child in a comprehensive care facility is about $5,600 per child per month. This is a very difficult position for states facing budget crises. While there are a number of reports on the various related issues, one study by ECPAT, "Who Is There to Help Us?" gives recommendations for developing a collective and cohesive voice in the

community to demand investigation and prosecu-
tion at all levels (local, state, and federal). Recommendations further included: development of
services for youth and education for those that
work with them, implementation of prevention
programs, and additional research on the issues.[1]

In the spring of 2012, the Department of Justice, Office of Juvenile Justice and Delinquency
Prevention convened a meeting in Salt Lake City
of experts working on the issue of domestic sex
trafficking and included several survivors of trafficking on a panel discussion. They had been
asked to tell the prosecutors, service providers,
and law enforcement in attendance what they believe were essential to assist victims of trafficking.
Here are their recommendations:

- All services are unconditional, not transac-
  tional
- Culturally appropriate support as needed
- Basic needs of safety, security, and survival
  come first
- Immediate needs include being treated
  with dignity and medical and psychological assistance

---

1 See the full report: http://ecpatusa.org/wp-content/
uploads/2010/11/Who-Is-There-to-Help-Us.3.pdf

- A safe, supportive environment and respectful climate is most effective
- Survivor advocates to assist through the process is important
  » Create opportunities to move from victim to survivor
  » Support networks that create cultural, psychological, and economic empowerment
  » Survivor opportunities to move back into society
  » A measure of self-determination over their own life
- Obtaining identification documents: birth certificate, driver's license, etc. to access available services
- Long-term needs to include:
  » Continuous therapy and support through systems and someone who is with them through the process
  » Life skills training to function in society
  » Drug and substance abuse training and treatment
  » Housing solutions
  » Education and job training
  » Access to affordable childcare

» Faith-based and community resources
» Immigration relief or assistance to return home for international families
» Victim-centered investigation that takes their needs into account
» Assistance with legal remedies for criminal records and credit histories

From this list of recommendations, you can see that the restoration of victims is a highly intensive and costly endeavor. There are models worth investigating if your goal or passion is to start a residential facility. Options exist for getting involved with organizations that already are at work. A partial list is included below.

Restoration from these exposures may take some time. Personal victimization or addiction issues must be addressed with a trusted counselor or with friends and family to mend the brokenness that has occurred. Children who have been sexually abused are resilient and they need caring adults in their lives to help them to find a measure of healing. Good children's advocacy centers and court appointed special advocates is a means to nurture children. Special training should be required to assist children through any of these channels.

Working with children extracted or rescued from commercial sexual exploitation requires a much more intensive and highly competent group of trauma-informed service providers. Models exist in the US and there is a movement of folks working toward the development of restoration facilities along the continuum of care of restoration. Most law enforcement and prosecutors are in need of centers that are secure for a debriefing time for the victims to understand the situation they are facing.

Law enforcement, prosecutors, and judges are at a loss for placement of these victims for several reasons.

1. Few options exist for residential placement in the US.
2. Most victims will not self-identify as victims and are resistant to assistance because the system has failed them so many times before or their pimp has told them he will beat or kill them for telling.
3. Many victims will choose to run from non-secure placement for several reasons in-

cluding abuse in foster care, training by their pimp to run, etc.

4. Victims have been arrested for some reasons and may have pending charges that would need to be addressed either related to their victimization or tangential to their victimization (i.e. their pimp had them stealing clothing or other items).

Juvenile Detention as Treatment

Treatment models for children who have been traumatized usually do not include incarceration. However, that is exactly what has been happening to many of these children. Several states have studies on children incarcerated with sexual abuse histories, some of which can be found online. In Texas a report compiled from several agencies for the legislature tells the story. Here are several of their key findings.

They recognized the system must get "upstream" on the river full of victims to begin to put the pieces together on the vulnerabilities of children to sexual exploitation. Here are three major factors to consider:[1]

---

1 https://www.ncjrs.gov/pdffiles1/ojjdp/NISMART.pdf

- Studies indicate that 25% of girls and 17% of boys will be sexually abused before their 18th birthday in the United States. (Stewards of Children)
- It is reported that 70% or more of the children who have been rescued from CSEC have been victims of sexual abuse. (Shared Hope)
- One extremely vulnerable population is the growing number of runaway and homeless children. The National Incidence Studies of Missing, Abducted, Runaway and Throwaway Children (NISMART) found that one out of every three runaway youth will be lured into prostitution within 48 hours of leaving home.

The study asked: What are the factors that contribute to child victims becoming detainees? The Texas report names three primary areas. Number 1 on their list is: identification barriers with five barriers to these children being appropriately identified. The report has graphics, which make it easier to visualize. The full report is available on line. The easiest issue to address is the lack of knowledge and training on the issues of Commercial Sexual Exploitation of Children (CSEC). The report goes on to identify legal barriers and services barriers in a similar pattern diagram (see pages 3 & 4). The report is very transparent of systemic issues and failures to identify these children.[1]

"Research indicates that the vast majority of juveniles engaging in prostitution are rarely identified as victims of sex trafficking. For those juveniles who are arrested for prostitution or identified as domestic victims of sex trafficking, limited resources are currently available within the community. What services are available depends on how the juvenile comes to the attention of authorities."[2]

This Texas study also identifies the vast chasms between agencies' assignments within the state. These include: Child Protective Services who work with the children of abuse; law enforcement agencies who arrest children for criminal offenses; Juvenile Detention system; and Juvenile Probation system. Each holds their portion of systemic failure to identify and provide treatment options outside of incarceration.

---

1   The full report is available at: http://www.tjjd.texas.gov/publications/reports/RPTOTH201103.pdf

2   Ibid (5).

While the report looks at alternative models in other states, Texas' legislative initiatives have continued to focus on penalties and statutes for perpetrators. There is a great need to incorporate the systemic changes necessary to implement a fundamental change as to how these children are dealt with from prevention to restoration.

Community education is key to developing a team of service providers and a unified approach along the continuum of care as recommended. Deena Graves and I have been able to provide education to educators, juvenile detention facilities, law enforcement, child abuse prevention advocates, national and state organizations that deal with children as well as civic groups and church communities.

To the best of my knowledge, there is no statewide plan at this time to facilitate the dissemination of information on CSEC. Some very small elements of CSEC are being included in the mandated training for law enforcement professionals, but there is no cohesive plan to bridge to all those mentioned in the continuum of care from the Department of Health and Human Services 2007 report.

We have a long way to go in getting this issue dealt with in a comprehensive manner. Groups that work on abuse prevention, especially sexual abuse prevention,[1] should be a part of an overall strategy to get "upstream" in the exploitation of children. There is a 2010 Department of Justice "national strategy" for addressing some of these issues. Unfortunately, there is a void between the information and the application of the strategy.[2] Considerable information is available about putting together a plan for communities and states.[3]

Communities should develop specialized outreach, education, and training programs to address gang-related trafficking. Prevention programs are an essential part of combating street gangs involved in human trafficking. New modules on street gangs can be added to anti-trafficking training courses and components on trafficking in persons must be added to street gang training. New educational curricula need to be developed for each classic concentric circle of concern: (a) the individual at risk, (b) family, (c) friends, (d)

---

1   www.stopitnow.org, www.d2l.org, www.ECPAT.org

2   http://www.projectsafechildhood.gov

3   A plan for Florida to address some of the issues for girls is available at: http://www.justiceforallgirls.org/advocacy/Bluprnt0109.pdf

schools, (e) religious institutions, and (f) communities. Each community should establish sector-specific training courses for parents, teachers, social workers, health providers, law enforcement officials, religious leaders, and others who may be first to encounter street gangs involved in human trafficking. Basic education about the problem is important; even more critical is a protocol for how to identify the problem and how to take immediate and effective action.[1]

The article "Finding A Path To Recovery: Residential Facilities For Minor Victims Of Domestic Sex Trafficking,"[2] is a good overview of the challenges and opportunities for those interested in developing or working with a residential facility. This brief focuses on minors who are victimized by sex traffickers across the US and the intent is to "provide practical information about the characteristic needs of these minors and describes the type of residential programs and facilities currently providing services for this population. The promising practices discussed here were identi-

---

1   Sold for Sex: The Link between Street Gangs and Trafficking in Persons by Laura J. Lederer (p. 19) The Protection Project Journal of Human Rights and Civil Society, Issue 4, Fall 2011.

2   Heather J. Clawson, Ph.D. and Lisa Goldblatt Grace

fied by directors and staff of residential facilities housing and serving minor victims of domestic trafficking, juvenile corrections facilities, programs for runaway and homeless youth, child protective services personnel, and law enforcement."[1]

Other locations not mentioned in the report above that are specifically faith-based include Wellspring Living in Georgia, New Day for Children in California, Street Light in Arizona, Gracehaven House in Ohio, and Salvation Army in Illionis.[2] There are other projects and homes affiliated with Shared Hope.[3] Baylor University Social Work students found 42 facilities that take sex

> *Whatever you do work at it with all your heart as working for the Lord, not for men. Since you know that you will receive an inheritance form the Lord as a reward. It is the Lord Christ you are serving.*
> *Col 3:23-24*

---

1   The series and the final study report can be downloaded from the following site: http://aspe.hhs.gov/hsp/07/HumanTrafficking/

2   http://www.wellspringliving.org/ http://www.newdayforchildren.com/ http://streetlightusa.org/life-house/ http://www.gracehavenhouse.org/ www.sapromise.org

3   http://www.sharedhope.org/WhatWeDo/RescueRestore/DomesticRescueRestoration/DomesticPartners.aspx

trafficking victims, most were for only adults. The Samaritan Women's organization has also compiled a list, some of which overlaps with Baylor's list but again most were for adults.[1]

Safe houses are being developed across the country. The ones I am most familiar with are in Texas. These include Houston (opened in 2012) Arrow Ministries' Freedom Place in cooperation

> *Do not be misled. Bad company corrupts good character.*
> *1 Corinthians 15:33*

with Children at Risk and Traffick911 has been gifted a location for Triumph House (Deena Graves, Executive Director). In East Texas there is Refuge of Flight (Norma Mullican, Executive Director) in cooperation with Buckner Children and Family Services of Dallas. In the San Antonio area there is the Freedom Youth Project and in Austin, Restore A Voice (Larry Megason, Executive Director.[2]

---

1 http://thesamaritanwomen.org/

2 http://www.freedomplace.us/site/freedom/home.html http://childrenatrisk.org/research/child-trafficking/ www.traffick911.com www.refugeoflight.org www.freedomyouthproject.org www.restoreavoice.org

There are new works in St. Louis, Missouri, Oklahoma City, Oklahoma, and others are being developed across the United States. Increased attention and the high demand for alternatives to juvenile detention through the judiciary have helped to foster a local response.

Studies of incarcerated youth indicate that many of them have been victims of exploitation and ended up in detention because of activities related to their victimization. They have been criminalized and not treated as victims. There are some very legitimate reasons for this approach and no good alternative has been standardized. There are judges who are proactively responding to this in Las Vegas, Nevada and in Houston, Texas with courts specifically addressing the girls' situations and looking for alternative options.

The work on this issue is about where we were with the issues of domestic violence 35 years ago. No shelters existed, the need was recognized, and people responded. You can look for work in your area and see if you can join them (use the HOPE matrix in this book) or if you need to begin a new work in your area.

Organizations like Abolition International are working on a credentialing for safe houses and on a manual of developing a home. They also have an annual conference and organizational membership for residential facilities. Wellspring Living in Georgia has a mentoring program for those that want to open safe houses. Freedom Place in Houston is working on a replication process for their organization as well.

Rules of Engagement

At a prayer event for human trafficking I was struck by the number of times that the women participating prayed that victims would have hope. This helped me to think about how true hope is an element that only the church can provide for prevention programs or the holistic recovery of victims.

The tangible articulation of hope is difficult. It is like the commercial of the children for the Ronald McDonald house. They are looking in their Happy Meal boxes for hope. The little boy says, "I know it's in there!"

Hope cannot be seen except in the eyes of someone who has found it. Programs can be developed in ways that foster hope, especially important is the true hope found in a relationship with Jesus Christ.

As a tangible means of seeing hope in an organization I developed this matrix. Ask God to show the organizations' true mission.

HOPE is an acronym matrix to use as a filter for assessing an organization with which you may engage or an endeavor that you may be called to develop with a critical and wise eye. These lists are a starting point and should not be considered an exhaustive evaluation instrument. You may have other questions you need to include.

H – Honors God

◊ Does the work (whether its mission is overtly Christian or not) function in a way that it values the people?

◊ Would their work be consistent with what you know about God's value of people?

◊ Are there elements that are contrary to Christian values and principles?

◊ Does it allow for faith as a piece of its programmatic elements?

◊ Does it allow for you to share your faith when asked or in an appropriate way?

You will need to know specifically what that means for each organization. I would caution you to not to be irresponsibly zealous.

◊ Is there any element of the program that is overtly anti-God, anti-Christ?

◊ Does the program require engagement in religion that is inconsistent with Biblical teachings?

◊ Do they communicate with clients and volunteers appropriately?

O – Operates With Ethics and Integrity

◊ Does the work hold a high standard as to the ethical treatment of its constituency?

◊ Is integrity integrated into their program, training, and communication pieces?

◊ Does the organization have high standards of financial accountability?

◊ What systems of accountability are in place for their staff?

◊ Do they perform training and resources for volunteers on ethics and integrity?

◊ Do they perform background checks on staff and volunteers, especially those that will be in contact with children?

◊ Do they require a confidentiality statement to be signed?

◊ Are there any elements in its programs that would lead you to believe they collaborate with organizations that are unethical or lack integrity?

◊ Simple things may be clues: do they open on time, answer phone calls and emails in a timely manner?

◊ Do they communicate with clients and volunteers in an ethical manner?

P – Purposefully Evaluates Itself

◊ Does the organization have a mission statement?

◊ How do they evaluate programmatic elements against the mission statement?

◊ Is there a systematic way of reporting issues with staff, volunteers, or clients?

◊ Do they hold regular meetings with staff and/or volunteers to make sure their objectives are being met?

◊ Do they conduct audits of their work-flow and assignments?

◊ Are there any on-going programs that are producing questionable results or expose problems in the elements that are not being addressed?

◊ Is there a mechanism to make suggestions or complaints?

◊ Are there processes for the leadership to help the organization stay on-task with daily operations?

◊ Do they have a budget and a plan to meet that budget?

◊ Are they always financially overextended or monitor and evaluate their expenses?

E – Empowers Their Constituency

◊ Does the organization have a planned approach to recruiting volunteers to be trained?

◊ Can trained volunteers represent the organization in the community?

◊ Does the organization certify or credential its volunteers or staff to make presentations on the organization's mission, vision, or operations?

◊ Is there a systematic way of reporting issues with staff, volunteers, or clients?

◊ Do they allow clients to make decisions and determine outcomes for themselves?

◊ Are their programs designed to create options for their clients in education?

◊ Can the clients choose a job skills or training program that fits their desires, gifts, and skills?

◊ Does the organization do things for the clients that they can do for themselves?

◊ Does the organization create client dependency rather than independence over time?

◊ Can clients choose or request different options for themselves?

◊ Are clients allowed to attend religious services of their own choice?

◊ Are clients offered physical and psychological services?

There are some highly competent organizations that meet many or most of these elements of evaluation. However, you will find that many passionate small organizations have not thought through many of these elements or are still in development. A keen attention to details will help you determine if the organization is going to be a one that you can work with or not. This should also help you if you plan to develop a nonprofit or ministry endeavor that brings tangible HOPE.

A Word of Caution

Any reputable organization that puts on event-based fund raising efforts in a local community should have grassroots engagement in that community. Several well-organized groups have done big events and raised lots of money in communities where they have no local groups that they work with or support with funding. This is detrimental to those organizations that are left behind in a community and left out of funding. People who give often think their funds go to support local efforts and it is not true. You would be wise to ask many questions about local partners and how the funds are distributed to them before you engage with these organizations.

When the Superbowl was hosted in Arlington, Texas, in February of 2011 the Arlington Police

Department reported 19 different NGO's showed up to intervene in the issues of sex trafficking. They were disruptive and detrimental relationally and financially for the local groups who were there before and long after the one-day event. Funding that could have helped tremendously was syphoned off by some of those organizations.

First Corinthians 3:13-15 should be an encouragement to build and evaluate the foundations of a program. Build your efforts in such a way that God is honored and the other three elements will surely follow the Master builders plumb line.

Arise, Lord! Lift up your hand, O God.
Do not forget the helpless.
Why does the wicked man revile God?
Why does he say to himself,
"He won't call me to account"?
But you, O God do see trouble and grief;
you consider it to take it in hand.
The victim commits himself to you;
you are the helper of the fatherless.
Break the arm of the wicked and evil man;
call him to account for his wickedness
that would not be found out.
The Lord is King for ever and ever;

the nations will perish from his land.
You hear, O Lord , the desire of the afflicted;
you encourage them, and you listen to their cry,
defending the fatherless and the oppressed,
in order that man, who is of the earth,
may terrify no more. (Psalm 10:12-18)

Our God sees what is happening, hears the cries of the children, and responds with compassion. His compassion draws us to the "burning bush" to experience what moves Him. He asks us to respond on His behalf. His strong and mighty hand will compel the release of the captives using us as His hands and feet to go.

How can we not take seriously our role, our God-given responsibility, and respond with the strength and compassion of our God as He directs our paths? It is not a matter of IF we should take our role seriously, we must! He has anointed us with the responsibility to live out Christ's mission. Jesus said in Luke 4:18-19 that his mission was, *"to preach good news to the poor, proclaim freedom for the prisoners and recovery of sight for the blind and to release the oppressed, and to proclaim the year of the Lord's favor."*

The Great Commandment should compel us to respond. *Love the Lord you Gods with all of our heart and with all your soul and with all your strength and with all your mind;' and 'Love your neighbor as yourself.* (Luke 10:27) We each have gifts, skills, talents, and abilities. He gave us those for His glory and His usefulness.

The most difficult part of responding is to love our enemies. Love must be extended to include those that are the offenders, the traffickers, the abusers, and those that pay to rape children. Jesus said in Luke 6:27, *"But I tell you who hear me: Love your enemies, do good to those who hate you; bless those who curse you, pray for those who mistreat you."* Loving your neighbor as yourself is difficult but loving your enemies is impossible unless God compels you.

Each of the wicked that perpetrate crime on other human beings will ultimately face judgment just as we will. Their deeds are not hidden from God and they will be accountable to Him. He is the final judge. Until

> *You may choose to look the other way, but you can never again say that you did not know."*
> ~ *William Wilberforce, 1789*

they stand before Him, we must believe there is hope for them to repent, turn from their wicked ways, and receive the gift of eternal life in Christ Jesus.

As for you, you were dead in your transgressions and sins, in which you used to live when you followed the ways of this world and of the ruler of the kingdom of the air, the spirit who is now at work in those who are disobedient. All of us also lived among them at one time, gratifying the cravings of our flesh and following its desires and thoughts. Like the rest, we were by nature deserving of wrath. But because of his great love for us, God, who is rich in mercy, made us alive with Christ even when we were dead in transgressions—it is by grace you have been saved. And God raised us up with Christ and seated us with him in the heavenly realms in Christ Jesus, in order that in the coming ages he might show the incomparable riches of his grace, expressed in his kindness to us in Christ Jesus. For it is by grace you have been saved, through faith—and this is not from yourselves, it is the gift of God—not by works, so that no one can boast. For we are God's handiwork, created in Christ Jesus to do good works, which God prepared in advance for us to do. Ephesians 2:1-10

It is possible for traffickers to turn from their wicked ways. One example of a slave trader who turned to Christ is John Newton. You may sing his song regularly and not know he had once perpetuated the slave trade in England. He eventually became a friend of abolitionist William Wilberforce. You see John found amazing grace in God's redemption and he wrote about it for all of the future generations to know that God saves wretches. Wretches like you and me. John wrote about it in "Amazing Grace" (A portion of the words are below.)

Amazing grace! How sweet the sound
That saved a wretch like me!
I once was lost, but now am found;
Was blind, but now I see.

'Twas grace that taught my heart to fear,
And grace my fears relieved;
How precious did that grace appear
The hour I first believed.

Through many dangers, toils and snares,
I have already come;

'Tis grace hath brought me safe thus far,
And grace will lead me home.
When we've been there ten thousand years,
Bright shining as the sun,
We've no less days to sing God's praise
Than when we first begun.

God saves us for His Glory and with a purpose to fulfill in our lives. Embrace God's design for you and fulfill your calling.

Take the challenge, join the movement, and fulfill your Ephesians 2:10 purpose.

> *For we are God's workmanship, created in Christ Jesus to do good works, which God prepared in advance for us to do.*
> *Ephesians 2:10*

Epilogue

If you are "ruined" by what you have read and are ready to take action with your life there are many avenues. I would be glad to assist you in finding the "on ramp" that fits your gifts, skills, talents, and abilities. No "one size fits all" will do when it comes to responding to God's call on your life. This must be a matter of concerted effort and prayer. The first thing that you must be sure of is your personal relationship to Christ.

If you do not know that you have come into a relationship with Jesus Christ that is the first and most important decision you can make in your life. It is not complicated. You acknowledge you are in need of him and you believe that Jesus Christ was who He said He was. You confess you are a sinner and accept His forgiveness. Read John

3:16 and ask Him to take over your life. Then, let the adventure begin!

The Bible will guide and direct you. Another book that helped me to nail down that decision and how to experience God in my everyday life is "Experiencing God" by Blackaby. Hearing God and knowing His voice is crucial to responding to human trafficking. Get the right relationship with Him first and everything else will fall in line. It will not be easy but it will be worth it!

You can stay in touch with updates on the materials and information coming out daily through the author's website and Facebook pages.[1]

---

1   www.tomigrover.com

Resources

Alford, D. "Free at Last: How Christians worldwide are sabotaging the modern slave trade," Christianity Today, February 21, 2007. http://www.christianityto-day.com/ct/2007/march/13.30.html

Arterburn, S., "Every Man's Battle" Colorado Springs, CO: Waterbrook, 2000.

Arterburn, S., "Every Young Man's Battle" Colorado Springs, CO: Waterbrook, 2000.

Bales, K. and Soodalter, R., The Slave Next Door: Human Trafficking and Slavery in America Today. Berkeley: University of California Press, 2009.

Bales, K., Disposable People: New Slavery in the Global Economy. Berkeley: University of California Press, 1999.

Bales, K., Ending Slavery: How We Free Today's Slaves. Berkeley: University of California Press, 2009.

Bales, K., Trodd, Z., Williamson, Alex K., Modern Slavery: the Secret World of 27 Million People. Oxford, England: Oneworld Publications, 2009.

Batterson, M. The Circle Maker. Grand Rapids, MI: Zondervan, 2011.

Batstone, D. Not For Sale: The Return of the Global Salve Trade. New York: Harper Collins Publishers, 2007.

Belles, N. In Our Backyard, self-published Free River, 2011.

Blackaby, H. Experiencing God, LifeWay, Nashville, 1990.

Clawson, J. Everyday Justice. Downers Grove, IL: InterVarsity Press, 2009.

Clawson, H.J. and Goldblatt Grace, L. "Finding A Path To Recovery: Residential Facilities For Minor Victims Of Domestic Sex Trafficking," http://aspe.hhs.gov/hsp/07/HumanTrafficking/

Driscoll, M. Porn-Again Christian. http://theresurgence.com/files/2011/03/02/relit_ebook_pac.pdf

End Child Prostitution, Pornography, and Trafficking (ECPAT). International Online Database, 22 March. http://www.ecpat.net, 2010.

Estes, R.J. and Weiner, N.A, The Commercial Sexual Exploitation of Children in the U.S., Canada and Mexico. Full Report of the U.S. National Study. Philadelphia: University of Pennsylvania, School of Social Work, Center for the Study of Youth Policy, 2001. http://www.sp2.upenn.edu/restes/CSEC_Files/Complete_CSEC_020220.pdf

Flores, Theresa, The Sacred Bath: An American Teen's Story of Modern Day Slavery. Lincoln: Universe, 2007. A second release goes by the title The Slave Across the Street - additions made to this edition.

Friedman, S, Who is There to Help Us? How the System Fails Sexually Exploited Girls in the United States. New York: ECPAT-USA, Inc., 2005. http://ecpatusa. org/wp-content/uploads/2010/11/Who-Is-There-to-Help-Us.3.pdf

Gray, G., Crowl, H., and Snow, K., "What's Our Responsibility? How Individuals and Organizations Can Proactively Address Human Trafficking," Journal of Applied Research on Children: Informing Policy for Children at Risk, Vol. 3, Iss. 1, Art. 20, February 24, 2012.

Haag, J. "Human Trafficking: The New Slavery," Therefore: Periodical of the Christian Life Commission of the Baptist General Convention of Texas, 7:1-7

Hughes, D.M., Best Practices to Address the Demand Side of Sex Trafficking, U.S. Department of State, 2004. http://www.uri.edu/artsci/wms/hughes/demand_sex_trafficking.pdf

Haugen, G., Good News About Injustice, Updated 10th Anniversary Edition: A Witness of Courage in a Hurting World. Downers Grove, IL: InterVarsity Press, 2009.

Haugen, G., Just Courage: God's Great Expedition for the Restless Christian, Downers Grove, IL: InterVarsity Press, 2008.

Haugen, G. and Hunter, G., Terrify No More: Young Girls Held Captive and the Daring Undercover Operation to Win Their Freedom (co-authored with Gregg Hunter) Nashville, TN: W Publishing Thomas Nelson, 2005.

Hughes, D.M., The Demand for Victims of Sex Trafficking, 2005. Available at: http://www.uri.edu/artsci/wms/hughes/demand_for_victims.pdf

Hughes, D.M., "Combating Sex Trafficking: A Perpetrator-Focused Approach." University Of St. Thomas Law Journal, 6(1):28-53, 2008.

Jewell, D. H., Escaping the Devil's Bedroom: Sex Trafficking, Global Prostitution, and the Gospel's Transformational Power, Grand Rapids, MI: Monarch Books, 2008.

Kreimeyer, V., Missions Mosaic, Go & Do Feature, "Human Trafficking in My Community? What Can I Do?" December 2010.

Lederer, L.J., Human Rights Report on Trafficking of Women and Children: A Country-by- Country Report on a Contemporary Form of Slavery. The Protection Project. Baltimore, MD: The Paul H. Nitze School of Advanced International Studies, Johns Hopkins University, 2001.

Lederer, L.J., Attacking Trafficking: U.S. Leadership in a Tri-Partite Approach to Addressing Supply, Demand, and Distribution, Chapel Hill, North Carolina: University of North Carolina International Conference On Sexual Trafficking: Breaking the Silence. April 7-8, 2006.

Lederer, L.J., Sold for Sex: The Link between Street Gangs and Trafficking in Persons, (p. 19) The Protection Project Journal of Human Rights and Civil Society, Issue 4, Fall 2011.

Levin, D and Jean Kilbourne, So Sexy So Soon New York: Ballantine Books, Random House, 2008. (http://dianeelevin.com/sosexysosoon/).

Malarek, V., The Natashas: Inside the New Global Sex Trade. New York: Arcade Publishing, 2004. (Note to reader R-Rated)

Malarek, V., The Johns: Sex for Sale and the Men Who Buy It. New York: Arcade Publishing, 2009. (Not to reader R-rated)

Mitchell, K.J., "Conceptualizing Juvenile Prostitution as Child Maltreatment: Findings from the National Juvenile Prostitution Study," Child Maltreatment, 15(1):18-36, 2010.

Mullican, N., and Zivney, M. A Collection of Squirrel Tales. Xulon Press, 2009.

Pearce, Q.L., Given Kachepa: Advocate for Human Trafficking Victims, KidHaven Cengage Publishing, 2007.

Piper, J. Don't Waste Your Life, Crossway Publishing, 2003.

Protocol to Prevent, Suppress, and Punish Trafficking in Persons, Especially Women, and Children, supplementing the United Nations Convention Against Transnational Organized Crime (i.e. "The Palermo Protocol), United Nations http://www.palermoprotocol.com/

Schapiro Group, Men Who Buy Sex with Adolescent Girls: A Scientific Research Study, 2010. http://afnap.org/wp-content/uploads/2010/06/The-Schapiro-Group-Georgia-Demand- Study.pdf

Schauer, E.J. & Wheaton, E.M., "Sex trafficking into the United States: A literature review," Criminal Justice Review, 31(2):146-169, 2006.

Schauer, E.J., Wheaton, E.M., and Galli, T. "Economics of Human Trafficking," (http://onlinelibrary.wiley.com/doi/10.1111/j.1468-2435.2009.00592.x/abstract).

Sher, Julian, Somebody's Daughter: The Hidden Story of America's Prostituted Children and the Battle to Save Them. Chicago: Chicago Review Press, 2011.

Sherman, B. Gregory's Paper Airplane, WestBow Press, 2010. http://gregoryspaperairplane.com/ The_Book.html

Skinner, E. B., A Crime So Monstrous: Face-to-Face with Modern-Day Slavery. New York: Free Press, 2008.

Smith, L. Renting Lacy, Shared Hope International. http://www.sharedhope.org/Resources/RentingLacy. aspx

Stearns, R., The Hole in the Gospel: What does God expect of the US? Nashville: Thomas Nelson, Inc., 2009.

Todres, J., "Taking Prevention Seriously: Developing a Comprehensive Response to Child Trafficking and Sexual Exploitation," Vanderbilt Journal of Transnational Law, Vol. 43, January, No.1, 2010. Electronic copy available at: http://ssrn.com/abstract=1544301

Todres, J., "Moving Upstream: The Merits Of A Public Health Law Approach To Human Trafficking," North Carolina Law Review, Vol.89, 447-ff. Electronic copy available at: http://ssrn.com/abstract=1742953

U.S. Department of Justice, The National Strategy for Child Exploitation Prevention and Interdiction, A Report To Congress, August 2010. http://www.justice. gov/psc/docs/execsummary.pdf

U.S. Department of State, Trafficking in Persons Report, 2012 (http://www.state.gov/g/tip/, June 2012.

Websites

A Heart for Justice, www.aheartforjustice.com.

ABC News, "Young Sexy," http://abcnews.
go.com/2020/video/young-sexy-15031065.

Acton University and Poverty Cure, www.povertycure.
org.

Better World Shopper, www.betterworldshopper.org

Chalmer's Institute, www.chalmers.org

Children at Risk, http://childrenatrisk.org/research/
child-trafficking/.

Christian Alliance for Orphans, www.christia-
nalliancefororphans.org.

Christian Community Development Association,
www.ccda.org.

Christian Medical Dental Association, CMDA: Trafficking in Persons: A Primer for the Health Care
Professional - Modules http://www.cmda.org/WCM/

CMDA/Navigation/Human_Trafficking/TIP_Module_
Descriptions.aspx.

Christian Women and Pornography www.Christian-
WomenandPorn.com/

Community and Restorative Justice, www.restorative-
justicenow.org.

CNN Freedom Project - http://thecnnfreedomproject.
blogs.cnn.com/2011/06/21/community-vigilance-
10-steps-people-can-take-to-help-combat-human-
trafficking/

Darkness to Light, "Stewards of Children," www.d2l.
org.

Department of Homeland Security, www.dhs.gov/
files/programs/human-trafficking-awareness-train-
ing.shtm).

Department of Justice, "Trafficking and Sex Tourism."
http://tinyurl.com/7xkv94q.

Department of Labor, www.dol.gov/

Enough is Enough, www.enough.org

Everyday Justice www.everydayjustice.net.

Federal Bureau of Investigation, "Crimes against Children." http://www.fbi.gov/hq/cid/cac/crimesmain.
htm.

Free 2 Work. "Corporate Responsibility, Slave Labor,
Watch List." http://www.free2work.org/home

Free the Captives, www.freethecaptiveshouston.org.

Free the Slaves. "Ending Slavery: The Twenty-five year plan." www.freetheslaves.net/SSLPage.aspx?pid=328.

Freedom Place, www.freedomplace.us/site/freedom/home.html

Freedom Youth Project, www.freedomyouthproject.org

Good News Goods, http://goodnewsgoods.com/

Gracehaven House, www.gracehavenhouse.org/

Holly Smith, http://hollyaustinsmith.com/.

Huffington Post "Nuns Concerned about Human Trafficking,"http://www.huffingtonpost.com/2012/01/18/nuns-concerned-about-human-trafficking-super-bowl_n_1213921.html.

Immokalee Farm Workers Union in Florida, (www.ciw-online.org/).

Initiative Against Sexual Trafficking, "What is the Initiative Against Sexual Trafficking?" www.iast.net/.

Institute of Medicine, http://www.iom.edu.

International Christian Alliance on Prostitutioin, http://www.icapglobal.org.

International Justice Mission, www.IJM.org.

Internet Safety 101, www.internetsafety101.org/101_video_clips.htm.

Interstate 10 Prayer Initiative, http://www.traffickstop.org/page/1010-for-i-10 or www.facebook.com/10at10forI10; news on this Initiative: http://www.baptiststandard.com/index.php?option=com_content&task=view&id=14318&Itemid=53

Law Enforcement Executive Forum, Vol. 12, No.1, March 2012 by John Vanek and Kirsten Foot. (http://traccc.gmu.edu/pdfs/Law_Enforcement_Executive_Forum.pdf#page=8)

The Lighthouse Network, http://lighthousenetwork.org/

Make Way Partners, www.makewaypartners.org.

Mariam Kagaso, http://kagasospeaks.webs.com/.

Morality in Media, www.moralityinmedia.org/

National Center for Missing and Exploited Children, http://www.ncmec.org/missingkids/servlet/PublicHomeServlet?LanguageCountry=en_US

National Child Traumatic Stress Network, www.nctsn.org/trauma-types/sexual-abuse

National Clearinghouse on Families & Youth, http://ncfy.acf.hhs.gov/book/export/html/131

New Day for Children, http://www.newdayforchildren.com/

Not for Sale, "Not For Sale: 27Million People are En-slaved Today." http://www.notforsalecampaign.org/

Passion Movement, www.268generation.com/3.0/.

Polaris Project: For a World without Slavery, "Com-bating Human Trafficking and Modern-day Slavery," www.polarisproject.org/.

Pornharms, http://pornharms.com/mim/handouts/

Prayer for Freedom, www.prayerforfreedom.com

Prism Magazine, http://issuu.com/prismmagazine/docs/jan-feb2012small_2, Vol. 19, No.1 "May I have a Word, Op-Ed, 2012

"Project Safe Childhood," www.projectsafechildhood.gov

PureHope, Providing Christian solutions in a sexual-ized culture, www.PureHope.net

Refuge of Light, www.refugeoflight.org.

Rescue and Restore, Given Kachepa's story: http://www.youtube.com/watch?v=bqyzW84I3Dc (at 6:42)

Restore a Voice, www.restoreavoice.org

The Samaritan Women, http://thesamaritanwomen.org/

Slavery Footprint, http://www.slaveryfootprint.org

Social Costs of Pornography, www.socialcostsofpornography.org/.

Somebody's Daughter, www.somebodysdaughter.com

Stop it Now, www.stopitnow.org.

Street Light, http://streetlightusa.org/life-house/

Strode, Tom. "Sex Trafficking." Faith and Family Values http://faithandfamily.com/magazine/article/sex-trafficking/.

Tampa Bay News, http://www.tampabay.com/news/publicsafety/crime/27-people-found-in-human-trafficking-raids-in-largo-clearwater/1138829

The Code, http://www.thecode.org

The Freedom Center in Cincinnati, OH, www.freedomcenter.org/.

Theresa Flores, www.traffickfree.com.

Trade As One, http://tradeasone.com/

Traffick911, www.traffick911.org

TraffickStop, http://www.traffickstop.org/page/advocate-policy-makers

Trans-Atlantic slave trade, www.slavevoyages.org/tast/index.faces.

UNICEF's 2008 report, http://www.worldhunger.org.

U.S. Department of Health & Human Services: Administration for Children & Families, "The Campaign to Rescue & Restore Victims of Human Trafficking. Free Resources. www.acf.hhs.gov/trafficking/.

Washington Post, "Toddlers and Tiaras" http://www.washingtonpost.com/blogs/celebritology/post/toddlers-and-tiaras-contestant-dresses-as-pretty-woman-prostitute/2011/09/07/gIQAErb78J_blog.html.

Wellspring Living, www.wellspringliving.org/

When Helping Hurts by Corbett and Fikkert, www.whenhelpinghurts.org.

World Crafts Village, www.worldcraftsvillage.com/.

World Vision, www.worldvision.org

WuDunn, Sheryl, TED Talk video: "Our century's greatest injustice," www.ted.com/talks/lang/eng/sheryl_wudunn_our_century_s_greatest_injustice.html

Articles -

http://www.tampabay.com/news/publicsafety/crime/27-people-found-in-human-trafficking-raids-in-largo-clearwater/1138829

http://www.polarisproject.org/resources/tools-for-service-providers-and-law-enforcement.

http://ecpatusa.org/wp-content/uploads/2010/11/Who-Is-There-to-Help-Us.3.pdf

http://www.tjjd.texas.gov/publications/reports/RP-TOTH201103.pdf

https://www.ncjrs.gov/pdffiles1/ojjdp/NISMART.pdf

http://www.justiceforallgirls.org/advocacy/Bluprnt0109.pdf

About the Author

Tomi Grover has been compelled to be involved in solving the human trafficking problem. She actively pursues educating others about the atrocities of exploitation and engages their response in a variety of avenues. Tomi teaches in the public arena for law enforcement, civic groups, schools, universities, and anywhere she has the opportunity. She holds a Doctor of Philosophy in Social Work and Ministry-Based Evangelism, and a Master of Arts in Christian Education, from Southwestern Baptist Theological Seminary.

www.tomigrover.com

Austin Brothers Publishing is a small publishing company that specializes in helping writers realize their dream of publishing a book. We can assist in any part of the process from having little more than an idea all the way to actually fulfilling orders for your printed book. As an author, you will work directly with editors and designers so the final product is a true reflection of what you intended. Our process is unique and allows the author to have a much greater share in the financial profit than with traditional publishers or other self-publishing models.

For more information visit our website – www.austinbrotherspublishing.com

CPSIA information can be obtained at www.ICGtesting.com
Printed in the USA
LVOW12s2118240813

349478LV00001B/2/P